The
#BlackLivesMatter
Movement

The
#BlackLivesMatter
Movement

Toward an Intersectional Theology

Edward Donalson III

CASCADE *Books* • Eugene, Oregon

THE #BLACKLIVESMATTER MOVEMENT
Toward an Intersectional Theology

Cascade Books
An Imprint of Wipf and Stock Publishers
199 W. 8th Ave., Suite 3
Eugene, OR 97401

www.wipfandstock.com

PAPERBACK ISBN: 978-1-7252-7183-8
HARDCOVER ISBN: 978-1-7252-7184-5
EBOOK ISBN: 978-1-7252-7185-2

Cataloguing-in-Publication data:

Names: Donalson, Edward, III, author.
Title: The #blacklivesmatter movement : toward an intersectional theology / Edward Donalson III.
Description: Eugene, OR: Cascade Books, 2021 | Includes bibliographical references.
Identifiers: ISBN 978-1-7252-7183-8 (paperback) | ISBN 978-1-7252-7184-5 (hardcover) | ISBN 978-1-7252-7185-2 (ebook)
Subjects: LCSH: Black lives matter movement. | Intersectionality (Sociology). | Theology—Methodology
Classification: BT738 D66 2021 (print) | BT738 (ebook)

JANUARY 7, 2021

This work is dedicated to my family members; they have made amazing sacrifices so support me on this journey. This work is also dedicated to every marginalized person whose personhood has been diminished and whose experience in this world has been made more difficult by imperialist, white-supremacist, capitalist, heteropatriarchy. Finally, this work is dedicated to The Fellowship of Affirming Ministries, without whom I would not have found this voice. Special thanks to John Malcomson for all your hard work with this project and as my Graduate Assistant.

CONTENTS

CHAPTER 1

INTRODUCTION

ON AUGUST 9, 2014, Darren Wilson—an officer of the Ferguson, Missouri, police department—murdered Michael Brown Jr. This was not the first murder of an unarmed Black man at the hands of an officer of the law in the United States, but it would become the spark to give life to a movement in America and beyond.

Michael Brown, an unarmed 18-year-old Black man, was killed in the middle of the day, in the middle of the street, in the middle of a residential community, and his body was left lying there for over four hours with his blood running in the streets for all to see.[1] There was something significant about the theme of the middle in Michael Brown's death: it thrust the Black male body in particular, and all Black bodies conceptually, into the middle of national conversation again.

At the time, I was pastor of a congregation of young men demographically connected to Michael Brown, so the similarities of this crime to the history of lynching in America was not in any way lost on me. These young men came of age politically with President Barak Obama in office, and now they bathed in the intense rage of Ferguson. In so many ways the lives of these young people were

1. Francis, *Ferguson and Faith*, 2.

unprecedented.[2] Many of them had been hypnotized by the myth of a post-racial society, and the shock of blatant racism unleashed a fear and rage in the congregation that had to be addressed. I realized suddenly that many of my congregants had embraced a mythology that our society was free from race-based bigotry, particularly the state-sanctioned type. That a government office could end life because of race-based fear or that the Black male body was culturally weaponized no matter who it is or the intention of the individual, was emotional and mental overload that needed to be addressed as a part of healthy spiritual care. The anti-Blackness of the American experience found an expression in the death of Mike Brown that was voiced on social media, impacting Michael Brown's contemporaries in ways they were unprepared to process.

The Canfield Green apartment community now became ground zero for the larger conversation between the imperialist, white-supremacist, capitalist, heteropatriarchy and a progressive, antiracist, anticlassist, antisexist, antiheterosexist political movement. It would not be long until, much like most lynchings in America, it would be announced that Michael Brown's murderer would never be charged—and ultimately no one would be held legally responsible for the death of this young man. The sustained invalidation of Black life is more than I, or the community, could stand to bear. What we didn't know in those moments immediately following Michael's death was that a string of murderous and dehumanizing invalidations lay ahead.

Returning to my congregation in the face of yet another refusal by the legal system to value Black lives would ultimately give birth to my own academic theopolitical investment in the #BlackLivesMatter movement. As a pastor, I knew I would need a theo-logic that spoke to the innumerable emotions swirling in the congregation and the wider community. The millennials in my congregation exhibited visible anger, while the seniors reacted with palpable dismay. The millennials communicated deep resentment for the System and fear for their lives, while the seniors' dismay carried with it a mandate to continue a fight they believed they

2. Glaude, *Democracy in Black*, 6.

had already won—or at least one they on which they had made progress. Dismay was rooted in the deconstruction of the belief that all of their marching and sitting in had indeed changed the hearts of the nation and not just the laws. The grief was so thick that it lasted a full year. Every time I thought it would lift and the congregation would have our collective breath again, a new victim of Blackness would arrive on our cell phones as proof that our terror was designed to keep us breathless.

At the turn of the twentieth century Black people began to transition from living largely in rural areas to starting new lives in predominantly urban settings. Since that time much has changed in Black life, in politics, and in the US culture; however, the threat and reality of police surveillance, scrutiny, violence, and even murder has remained remarkably consistent.[3] It seemed in those days following Michael Brown's death that the treatment of his body at the scene of his murder was an intentional warning designed to strike fear in our hearts and remind us of our already hyper-visibility as we navigated through the commons. As I looked into the faces of the people I was charged to serve, in each set of eyes I saw questions about how our faith can inform our circumstances. The task of the Black theologian (particularly the pastoral theologian) is to wake up the dead, and by that I mean we are called to wake up subjectivity, notions of agency, identity, and human flourishing, in conversation with resistance and self-love.[4] These, however, are not the particular circumstances that originally gave birth to #BlackLivesMatter. The inception of the movement involved a young man in a similar situation named Trayvon Martin, whose story I had previously addressed within our congregation. But Michael Brown and his execution birthed my deep passion to put the movement in conversation with theology. Michael Brown's death was the tipping point for our community; for us, God had to be relevant and present in new and living ways. The blood of Michael Brown cried out from the streets and would not be ignored.

3. Taylor, *From #BlackLivesMatter to Black Liberation*, 107.
4. Fluker, *Ground Has Shifted*, 21.

As a son of the Black Church, I am motivated to contribute to the sustainability of social movements that have high impact on the life of the church. Currently there is a failure of the church to engage theologically with contemporary social movements. In this social media age, the church needs to engage in ways that foster sustainability for generational understanding. This is particularly true in the case of the #BlackLivesMatter movement. As I consider how the church can give specific theo-logic and theological language to the movement that will be sustainable in the long run, I am energized by the opportunity to be a part of shaping the conversation that will offer theological significance. I am equally enthused by the language that the #BlackLivesMatter movement offers to the God-Talk of the Black Church. There is an opportunity at this moment in history to see firsthand the working reciprocity between community and the theology it shapes. Theology is always engaged with voices from communities that give meaning to the text and language to the concepts revealed in the text. Once the language has been provided, the church can begin to engage the movement, or at a minimum to understand its disengagement from this particular movement—thereby making the movement serve as a prophetic critique of the church's capacity.

The task of theology is to critique and revise the language of the church. This includes not only the language of uttered speech, but also the language of radical involvement in the world.[5] Theology is always political, and the #BlackLivesMatter movement is one of the most important theopolitical movements of our time. Politics is the ancient and honorable endeavor to create a community in which the weak as well as the strong can flourish, where love and power can collaborate, and justice and mercy can have their day.[6] By its nature, including its social engagement and praxis, the #BlackLivesMatter movement is both a political and theological movement. It is a movement of radical solidarity not born from political theory, but rather out of a shared, lived experience and circumstance. #BlackLivesMatter is more than a

---

5. Cone, *Black Theology and Black Power*, 84.
6. Palmer, *Healing the Heart of Democracy*, 8.

slogan; it is indeed a movement because—based on its tenets—it seeks action. Black persons across the spectrum of society are not a monolith, but there is at this time in history enough shared trauma to ignite a shared passion for action. There is in this moment a need for change, as the status quo has become too unbearable for the majority of people. Movements are not mere intellectual pursuits; they are primarily concerned with how one changes the system.[7] It is our task, as practitioners of the sacred, to assist people in plumbing the depths of their own humanity, where transcendence, mystery, being, and even love are discovered, and then to bring those qualities found in the center of life into the world.[8]

Critique of the church is conducted in light of the gospel narrative of Jesus' life and the tradition of gospel values as seen in the biblical text. Serving as I do as a bishop in the Lord's Church, I understand that the work of doing public theology is a fundamental part of the vocation. God-talk, for the Christian, is the font of civic action. Matters of society and justice are never separate from religion, because it is our religion that compels us to work toward a more just and humane world. Beginning in the twelfth year of my episcopacy and the first year as Presiding Prelate of The United Ecumenical College of Bishops, this work put into context my understanding of the meaning and value of religion which, for me, is determined by how well it meets the needs of the disinherited.[9] This book will be a vehicle to engage the academy, the church, and the public simultaneously around the issue of human rights. The opportunity for a bishop—specifically in the Pentecostal tradition—to speak in a scholarly way to a social movement, as it is taking shape, is an opportunity not often maximized. As a constructive theologian with a liberative lens, I am excited by the opportunity that the #BlackLivesMatter movement offers the church to evaluate where our language and praxis both portray and betray the gospel narrative.

7. Fromm, *On Being Human*, 59.

8. Spong, *Why Christianity Must Change*, 166.

9. My understanding of the disinherited is greatly influenced by the work of Howard Thurman. Thurman, *Jesus and the Disinherited.*

As a religious scholar, I must admit that I struggle with the idea that theology is a purely distinct mode of thought. This Western Anglo-Teutonic insistence upon a categorical distinctive suggests that there is somehow a divide between sacred and secular. For me this insistence must be questioned: What counts, and who decides what counts, as theological thought? The theologian's very identity is produced through the capacity to "think theologically" as a pure category, as a distinct mode of thought.[10] What I propose is that all thoughts are in some way connected to God-Talk, and so throughout this book I will lift streams of theology to be considered as a part not only of theological discourse, but all discourse. It is my contention that a theology that does not work within the context of a holistic view of reality cannot address the needs of our time.[11] We need a theo-logic that helps us make sense of and respond to the insanity of imperialist white supremacist capitalist heteropatriarchy and all other systems of domination that serve to disenfranchise and marginalize any of the beloved of God.

When I began writing, the #BlackLivesMatter movement had thirteen published tenets inclusive of, but not limited to, restorative justice, queer affirming, and unapologetically Black.

TENETS OF THE #BLACKLIVESMATTER MOVEMENT

DIVERSITY

We are committed to acknowledging, respecting, and celebrating difference(s) and commonalities.

GLOBALISM

We see ourselves as part of the global Black family and we are aware of the different ways we are impacted or privileged as Black folk who exist in different parts of the world.

10. Crawley, *Blackpentecostal Breath*, 15.
11. McFague, *Models of God*, 14.

BLACK WOMEN

We are committed to building a Black women-affirming space free from sexism, misogyny, and male-centeredness.

BLACK VILLAGES

We are committed to disrupting the Western-prescribed nuclear family structure requirement by supporting each other as extended families and "villages" that collectively care for one another, and especially "our" children to the degree that mothers, parents, and children are comfortable.

LOVING ENGAGEMENT

We are committed to embodying and practicing justice, liberation, and peace in our engagements with one another.

RESTORATIVE JUSTICE

We are committed to collectively, lovingly, and courageously working vigorously for freedom and justice for Black people and, by extension, all people. As we forge our path, we intentionally build and nurture a beloved community that is bonded together through a beautiful struggle that is restorative, not depleting.

COLLECTIVE VALUE

We are guided by the fact that all Black lives matter, regardless of actual or perceived sexual identity, gender identity, gender expression, economic status, ability, disability, religious beliefs or disbeliefs, immigration status, or location.

EMPATHY

We are committed to practicing empathy; we engage comrades with the intent to learn about and connect with their contexts.

QUEER AFFIRMING

We are committed to fostering a queer-affirming network. When we gather, we do so with the intention of freeing ourselves from the tight grip of heteronormative thinking or, rather, the belief that all in the world are heterosexual unless s/he or they disclose otherwise.

UNAPOLOGETICALLY BLACK*

We are unapologetically Black in our positioning. In affirming that Black Lives Matter, we need not qualify our position. To love and desire freedom and justice for ourselves is a necessary prerequisite for wanting the same for others.

TRANSGENDER AFFIRMING

We are committed to embracing and making space for trans brothers and sisters to participate and lead. We are committed to being self-reflexive and doing the work required to dismantle cis-gender privilege and uplift Black trans folk, especially Black trans women who continue to be disproportionately impacted by trans-antagonistic violence.

BLACK FAMILIES

We are committed to making our spaces family-friendly and enable parents to fully participate with their children. We are committed to dismantling the patriarchal practice that requires mothers to work "double shifts" that require them to mother in private even as they participate in justice work.

INTERGENERATIONAL

We are committed to fostering an intergenerational and communal network free from ageism. We believe that all people, regardless of age, show up with capacity to lead and learn.

Coined by BYP100.[12]

These tenets make clear that the #BlackLivesMatter movement sits at the intersection of race, sex, gender, and religion. These tenets speak to embodiment, which has been a site of trouble for Black bodies from the time of chattel slavery forward. These tenets are well articulated, but do not read as distinctly

12. BlackLivesMatter, "About Page."

theological. This book attempts to tease out the operative theology of #BlackLivesMatter and offer the #BlackLivesMatter movement, and pastors of local congregations, the theological vocabulary and concepts to advance their dialogue. I do not claim to speak on behalf of the #BlackLivesMatter movement or even from the movement. My work here is to speak from the Black church to the movement and from the movement to the Black church. I also understand that while these tenets must be articulated in theological terms, if the theological method of Black and womanist theologians does not provide a bridge between liberationist God-talk and the practice of ministry, numbers of churches will succumb to white evangelicalism with no prophetic action.[13] In many cases, the history of Puritanism and the extreme privileging of evangelicalism in the Black Church have drowned out the prophetic critique that enables the Black Church to be useful in dismantling imperialist, white-supremacist, capitalist, heteropatriarchal norms in society. Puritanism in America leaves the Black Church a fourfold inheritance of terror. The legacy is a theological threat to safety in the way it positions the Black person to dread God and God's blazing hell.

Puritanism also poses a sociological/racial threat to safety for a Black person in a racist society informed by a theology of white superiority. It further presents a sexual threat to safety that stems from a sense of personal corruption and spirit/body duality.

Finally, Puritanism is a gendered threat to safety for the damage done to both Black women and men by its extreme patriarchy.[14] The relationship between the theological infrastructure of a faith community and its social manifestations is circular, each influencing the other.[15] #BlackLivesMatter provides these theologies with a vehicle of active agency in the world. #BlackLivesMatter is a psycho-sexual-religious-rebellious protest and must, therefore, belong to theological conversation in a very tangible way. This vehicle is only useful provided that the pastors of local congregations

13. Warnock, *Divided Mind,* 112.

14. Kornegay, *Queering of Black Theology,* 24.

15. Warnock, *Divided Mind,* 114.

are compelled, by the theology present in the documented infra-structure of the movement, to encourage parishioners to support and engage in the life of the movement.

I begin this book by stating the problem that is the focus of examination, as well as offering an explanation about the purpose of the work. Next, I name the research questions, the concep-tual frameworks, and the importance of the conversation. This includes a reflection on the theological streams that impact the overall conversation. Following the theological reflection, the next chapter lays out the methodology. I then elucidate my findings of the study and close with my final conclusions that look forward to what should be done in light of the experience.

If there is a failure of the Black Church to theologically en-gage contemporary social movements in the social media age, this is particularly true for the #BlackLivesMatter movement. How can the Black Church offer specific theological language to this move-ment? How can the #BlackLivesMatter movement serve as critique of the theological language and praxis of the church? Movements are benefited and become sustainable when they have ideological, sociological, and theological underpinnings. This book will help name the God claims implicit in #BlackLivesMatter. The particu-larity of these Black lives can then inform the aggregate lives of all of Christendom and ultimately the conversation about gospel values in society. I am clear that the focus of this project is the impact of #BlackLivesMatter on Black church life, and it is counter hegemonic. While some seek to make #BlackLivesMatter, and the theology that undergirds it, of import to the dominant culture, my particular focus is to center Blackness as important irrespective of white gaze. This is not a book to engender white guilt. White guilt is unhelpful. What we need in this epoch of time is white responsibility. What will the dominant culture do with its privilege in light of the gospel narrative? When I speak of whiteness in this work, it is not a skin color, because the parameters of whiteness change historically. When I speak of whiteness I speak of the social construct of power and domination rooted in anti-Blackness, that serves to disinherit and marginalize those considered radically other. Race is not a concrete or static reality, but an imaginative construct created in particular times and places by specific influences and impacts.[16]

From the onset of our history in this nation, Black people recognized a link between reading, critical thinking, and self-actualization. This recognition has been constantly under assault by the dominant culture in an effort to maintain its privilege. Black writers and thinkers in academe, like all marginalized groups, are constantly subjected to pejorative scrutiny, especially when the subject is resistance to privilege norms.[17] While there is in America a culture of fascination which focuses on whiteness as normative and centers whiteness as the subject, this book is not primarily concerned with whiteness, rather in the voices from the margins coming into the center as full members of the global community.

My intention is to explore the tenets of the #BlackLivesMatter movement in dialogue with a specific set of God claims. To discover ways to prompt a conversation about how this generation views embodiment as connected to the divine would go a long way to further the message of Christ. I see this work as a catalyst to a larger body of work that puts the church, the academy, and the public in ongoing dialogue specifically addressing the forward movement of human flourishing. It is clear that more work must be produced in Black Studies and every other discipline, toward creating a more just and humane world where Black bodies are no longer demonized and criminalized. Black Studies is the force of belief that Blackness is but one critical and urgently necessary disruption to the epistemology, the theology-philosophy, that produces a world, a set of protocols, wherein Black flesh cannot clearly breathe.[18] White-supremacist thinking, rooted in metaphysical dualism, socialized citizens of this nation to think in binaries such as good/bad and black/white. This has been the ideological rationale for the domination permeating our nation's

16. Hill Fletcher, *Sin of White Supremacy*, 3.

17. hooks, *Yearning*, 10.

18. Crawley, *Blackpentecostal Breath*, 3.

religious thought and shaping its most powerful institutions.[19] Racist ideas rooted in racist theo-logic make people who are not of the dominant culture think less of themselves, while making white people think more highly of themselves, which further attracts them to racist ideas.[20] The #BlackLivesMatter movement is a means to opening a fresh theological conversation on how to dismantle this damaging paradigm.

Clearly the #BlackLivesMatter movement is not an end in itself; it is a means to an end and a stage in the process of human flourishing. This book opens the door to facilitate discussions about the movement through a theological lens and to provide the God claims in front of audiences with the ability to impact the broader community. It serves as a tool for navigating the complex intersection of race, sex, gender, and religion in the life of the church and the whole Black community.

I also intend to impact those in the center of power by lifting scholarship around the #BlackLivesMatter movement in a way that institutionalizes it. Simply by writing about a cultural movement, grants that movement the perception of a new level of social legitimacy. I see this project as imperative to lifting voices that are often overlooked or undervalued in academic and public discourse. It also makes a difference to future students of the movement when work has been done regarding the movement by someone of the same demographic. There is a certain voice that the dominant culture brings to the study of Black movements and this is an opportunity for me as a Black theologian and academic to offer at least a particular Black voice. Lending to the sustainability of any movement is its capacity to articulate itself—for itself and for others and/or to be articulated by those it seeks to redeem.

Social movements need an ideological, sociological, and theological framework to ensure its longevity, and this book highlights the theological framework while allowing the articulation of the movement simultaneously. The interventions created by the civil rights struggle, and the movements of militant Black

19. hooks, *Rock My Soul*, 202.

20. Kendi, *How to Be an Antiracist*, 6.

resistance to white supremacy effectively raised consciousness and helped many Black people divest themselves of internalized white-supremacist assumptions about the ugliness of Black bodies.[21] The #BlackLivesMatter movement, underscored by theological context, stands to further this work of reimagining the sacred worth of Black bodies. As our bodies are always in this society raced, gendered, and sexed along with other qualifiers, it is important to address how the tenets of #BlackLivesMatter serve to (re)member those bodies into wholeness. The critical task of remembering includes the weeping, confessing, and resistance, but distances itself from any critique that has the effect of undermining the liberative yearnings of Black life.[22]

The purpose of this basic qualitative research study is to articulate the intersections of womanist, Black liberation, and queer theologies within the #BlackLivesMatter movement in the US. The particulars of the multiple-burdened founders of the movement lend themselves easily to these theological lenses, and the movement that has grown is intentionally inclusive of those who reflect the realities that bring these theological streams together. #BlackLivesMatter was created by three Black queer women, Alicia Garza, Opal Tometi, and Patrisse Cullors, in the wake of George Zimmerman's trial for the killing of Trayvon Martin.[23] The lived realities and intersectionality of these women show up in the core tenets as a prescriptive call for social justice and a rethinking of the very constructs of our society. There is nothing tentative or hesitant about the tenets of #BlackLivesMatter, they leap from the page as a manifesto of love and liberation for the least of these. They call for the revolutionary idea of the death of anti-Blackness. Without erasing difference the tenets of the #BlackLivesMatter movement invite Black people to self-love expressed in self-care and neighbor love. They hold love as an intricate part of justice, which is the public manifestation of love. They speak to the dominant culture a demand which is the failure to acknowledge it

21. hooks, *Salvation*, 60.

22. Fluker, *Ground Has Shifted*, 40.

23. Lightsey, *Our Lives Matter*, 66.

as power. #BlackLivesMatter never directly addresses a demand to the dominate culture which is to decenter whiteness as normative and speak to the subjectivity of the Black body and life. This movement and its tenets are a declaration of war on the status quo. It attacks the interlocking systems of oppression that dominate and terrorize minoritized and marginalized communities. The call to action is a new social contract that remakes relations of power.

The failure of the Black Church to theologically engage contemporary social movements in the social media age is particularly relevant in the case of the #BlackLivesMatter movement. How can the Black Church offer specific theological language to this movement? Movements are benefited and become sustainable when they have ideological, sociological, and theological underpinnings; this book, therefore, will help name the God claims implied in #BlackLivesMatter. The particularity of these Black lives then informs the aggregate lives of all Christendom.

The Black Church carries the unwritten negative symbolism of Puritanism, as can be seen in the sexisms and homophobias that are prevalent today. The Black Church has been used to dispense puritanical proscriptions against Black bodies, and the tenets of #BlackLivesMatter serve as liberative antidotes to this long-standing narrative.[24] As Evangelicalism gained popularity in much of the Black Church in America, the historic anti-Blackness of the Evangelical church found its way into the Black pulpits. Historical amnesia swept through many pulpits as the preachers forgot that the Evangelical church supported the status quo. Pro-slavery, pro-segregation, anti-interracial marriage, or any other attempt at personhood and flourishing have been the hallmarks of Evangelicalism in America and yet it is that very same theo-logic that has been the root of much preaching and practice in many Black church spaces.

I am extremely passionate about seeing the kinship of humanity realized, but I realize this vision of ultimate unity hinges on healing for all groups of people. Before the Kindom (a purposeful renaming of Kingdom, without the tainting language

24. Kornegay, *Queering of Black Theology*, 48.

of empire. This language is a gift to us from womanist scholars.) of God is manifested on the earth, the disparate parts of humanity must be made whole. Marginalized people are damaged by those in the center of power; hence,the damage caused to those on the underside of power must be addressed. The damage caused to marginalized people begins to be repaired by a theological response to the brokenness of humanity. The ongoing subservience to European models of Jesus damages the psychological health of Blacks, who face racism in a society where the overwhelming majority of authority figures and people with power are white.[25] We need a progressive transformative vision of social justice that will combine the wisdom of a successful nonviolent, love-based freedom struggle with the insights of a direct-action, decolonizing movement for Black self-determination and liberation. I am convinced that this is the ethic of the #BlackLivesMatter movement.[26]

I surveyed four Black, academically trained theologians in Black, womanist, and queer theologies using a set of open-ended questions that are in conversation with the tenets of the #Black-LivesMatter movement. These surveys were conducted in writing. I then provided a rubric for a theological discussion that ultimately puts the #BlackLivesMatter movement in dialogue with the wider Black Christian communion by forming a focus group of Black pastors who lead Black congregations. These congregations are members of the historically Black Christian denominations formed in response to the realities of slavery and racism. Exactly in the way that Rev. Dr. King and Rev. Thurman provided a robust theological framework for the civil rights movement that expanded during the span of the movement, so must modern scholars serve modern movements in the same way.

Probes were prepared for the survey and room for unanticipated probes was built in. To determine the impact of the data collected by the surveys, I also convened a focus group of pastoral leaders from across the nation. The focus group was made up of

25. Hopkins, *Introducing Black Theology*, 63.
26. Content based on the writing of bell hooks; hooks, *Salvation*.

pastors who are actively serving African American congregations across the country and who meet annually at the Love Fellowship Music and Arts Conference. Pastors can sign up to participate in sessions each day and this focus group was offered as one of the sessions the pastors could opt into during the 2016 Music and Arts Love Fellowship Conference held in Lombard, Illinois.

CHAPTER 2

THEOLOGICAL REFLECTION

FOR ME, AS A constructive theologian (I am not in pursuit of a systematic theology nor the work that theology has been, rather my work is centered in trying to understand what a viable faith can be in the present in light of the traditions of the past) with a liberative lens, Christian theology is language about God's liberating activity in the world on behalf of the oppressed. Any talk about God that fails to make God's liberation of the oppressed its starting point is not Christian.[1] This work of liberation theology is done by looking at the praxis of the person Jesus and the values that can be connected with his life and work. The biblical text suggests that Jesus possessed a perfect ministerial vision of righting relationships between body (individual and community), mind (of humans and tradition), and spirit. Liberation theology takes seriously the nonnormative body of Jesus, who is God in flesh, and places it in conversation with the project of decentering the embodiment of the dominant culture as normal.[2] God-talk based on a preferential posture to the least of these, those on the margins, is rooted in an ethic of radical neighbor love. This is the center of my understanding of what it means to be distinctly Christian.

1. Cone, *Speaking the Truth*, 4.
2. Turman, "Conversation with Dr. Turman."

Within each set of social relations in US society and culture, there is an imbalance of power. Hegemony maintains this inequality and is seen as normal and right. It also works to keep the dominant group in power by promoting its worldview as neutral, universal, normative, and right. This works so that those who have no power see the world in the same way as those with power.[3] Liberation theology is not the work of systematic theology, particularly because systematic theology is often a way that church intellectuals keep sexuality from the ambiguous, polymorphic expressions— that "others" press and sublimate—that would otherwise open new vistas on Divinity. In most systematics, heteronormativity[4] is tightly woven with colonialism and the silencing of non-Euro, non-modern, non-capitalist "others."[5] The project of liberation theology decenters whiteness as normative and disallows those who believe themselves to be white to control the gospel narrative. I say here those who believe themselves to be white because whiteness is a shifting, moving, unstable category. Whiteness has variable criteria in the American experiment at different moments in time, rooted only in the service of excluding non-white others.[6] Racial exclusion was designed to protect the elite heteropatriarchy of native-born whites. In the racial logic of the nation state, immigrants and other nonwhite bodies were racialized as the antithesis of heteropatriarchal ideals. Race as an American institution is an invitation to power and privilege or excommunication and exclusion from that same power and privilege. The construct of race is built to identify proximity to power. As ethnicity and social construction were invented racial exclusion and ethnic assimilation provided the genealogical context for sociology's inscriptions of race and sexuality as socially constructed.[7] The proclamation of the

---

3. Townes, *Blaze of Glory*, 72.

4. By this I mean both those localized practices and those centralized institutions that legitimate and privilege heterosexuality and heterosexual relationships (Johnson and Henderson, *Black Queer Studies*).

5. Crawley, *Blackpentecostal Breath*, 14.

6. Hill Fletcher, *Sin of White Supremacy*, 3.

7. Johnson and Henderson, *Black Queer Studies*, 56.

Word of life demands the transformation of tradition so that life can be lived more abundantly.[8] To express a God of liberty rather than a God of domestication, it is central to liberation theologies that they use social analysis to expose systems of domination such as colonialism, militarism, racism, and sexism.[9]

The ethos of the ministry of Christ was constantly befriending the friendless and identifying himself with the underprivileged. According to the New Testament (Luke 4:18–19), Jesus' self-proclaimed mission is inexplicable apart from others. Others, of course, are all people, particularly the oppressed and unwanted of society. Here is God coming into the depths of human existence for the sole purpose of striking off the chains of slavery, thereby freeing humanity from the ungodly principalities and powers that hinder people's relationship with God.[10] The creation of the radical "other" is always a gateway to evil. Not just identifying that which is different, the creation of the other is a work of dehumanization. The despised other is someone who has become so alien to you that all manner of disenfranchisement is justifiable, because they cease to hold the status of human. The earliest generations of Christian thinkers saw the incarnation of God in Jesus Christ was so that all persons might become "incarnated" in the eternal life of the Trinity.[11]

As Jesus becomes a friend to outcasts (Matt 11:19), inviting them to eat with him, he epitomizes the scandal of inclusiveness for his time. What is manifested in his healing of the sick is pushed to an extreme in Luke 11 by his invitation to the ritually unclean to dine with him.[12] Even the crucifixion of Christ models the praxis of his ministry in that it most clearly and radically identifies Jesus with the slave community. It forged an inextricable bond between the two. Through the cross Jesus' suffering and the slaves' suffering

8. Williams, *Sisters in the Wilderness*, 165.

9. Hennelly, *Liberation Theologies*, 96.

10. Cone, *Black Theology and Black Power*, 35.

11. Buechel, *That We Might Become God*, 2.

12. McFague, *Models of God*, 52.

of his era and all times become one.[13] The life and praxis of Jesus then does three things: (1) reflects an intimate relationship between Jesus and the oppressed;(2) radicalizes the oppressed to fight for their freedom; and (3) highlights the contradiction between the divine and the oppressor.

#BlackLivesMatter is an important social transformation movement, not only for Black people but for the whole of US society. It echoes the themes of dignity of the Black Power movement for the Black community and speaks truth to the power of the dominant culture. It is true that talk about liberation becomes hard to justify where freedom appears as nothing more than defiant self-assertion of a revolutionary racial consciousness that requires for its legitimacy the opposition of white racism. However, it is also true that we are in a historical moment that demands opposition to imperialist, white-supremacist, capitalist, heteropatriarchy.[14] The struggle for liberation that befalls Black Americans is the salvation of themselves and our oppressors simultaneously. The oppressor can only be liberated from the evil of oppression when the oppressed cast off the dehumanization of oppression.[15] The unfair burden of liberating one's oppressors means that for the whole of society Black lives indeed do matter because it is the struggle for humanization of the Black life that serves to deliver whiteness from its excessive evil.

The imperialist, white-supremacist, capitalist, heteropatriarchy is the set of interlocking political systems that form the foundation of our nation's politics.[16] The health of American society depends on facing and dealing with the issues #BlackLivesMatter names. The aim and structure of good theological endeavors should arise from an analysis and experience of the undertaking for full humanity in the anthropological and ecological interactions in the world.[17] Good theology is transgressive in that it seeks to challenge

---

13. Douglas, *Black Christ*, 21–22.

14. See Sanders, "Problem of Irrelevance," 73–82.

15. Freire, *Pedagogy of Freedom*, 44.

16. hooks, *Will to Change*, 17.

17. Hopkins, *Black Faith and Public Talk*, 42.

social norms where they are contrary to human flourishing. #BlackLivesMatter is a movement founded by Black people who love Blackness; that is, they have decolonized their minds and broken with the kind of white-supremacist thinking that suggests that Black people are inferior, inadequate, and unworthy; by doing so they call all Black people and the nation as a whole into this place of freedom.[18] The anti-Black theo-logic entrenched in the founding of this nation results in anti-Black public policy and the legalization of marginalization, thus #BlackLivesMatter is a theopolitical antidote to the theopolitical sickness of institutionalized racism.

This chapter looks at the theological foundations of this book. It investigates the nature of Black liberation theology, womanist theology, and queer liberation theology and how the #BlackLives-Matter movement embodies those culturally embedded theologies. Further, the chapter explains the theological foundations for pursuing the work and identifies the streams of theology that impact an understanding of the work. Finally, the chapter also indicates the primary sources used as conversation partners informing the theo-logic presented.

Reinhold Niebuhr, one of the premier theologians of the twentieth century, is the perfect example of a public theologian. As an intellectual, he participated in public discourse in ways that intentionally brought gospel values to the conversation. Niebuhr interpreted certain historical and political problems by focusing on how the need for power is part of human nature and sinfulness.[19] This is the duty of the theologian, to bring to light where the church is both portraying and betraying the gospel narrative. Sallie McFague, a prolific feminist theologian, taught that if one understands the life and death of Jesus as a parable of God's relation to the world, then being a Christian means to be willing to look "God-wards" through the Jesus story. Further, one is constrained to ask how that story is significant now.[20] This is of

18. hooks, *Black Looks*, 17.

19. West, *Disruptive Christian Ethics*, 22.

20. McFague, *Models of God*, 7.

great import in that what makes theology distinctively Christian is its analysis in light of the person and work of Jesus.

Theology as an art and science is confessional, for the theologian (as exegete, prophet, teacher, preacher, and philosopher) must clarify the church's faith in relation to its participation in God's liberating activity in the world.[21] Viable theology has a reciprocal relationship with the community with which it interacts, and the current sociopolitical climate in the United States demands extensive liberation theology with a resistance edge. Not only the community matters, but the theologian as person matters. The theologian writes from their own location to an audience for a purpose and this can never be overlooked. One must be aware of who is writing, the message they wish to convey, and why the messenger feels compelled to deliver the message.[22] The theo-logic of the theologian is always impacted by the particulars of that theologian to one degree or another. One's work is never incidental to one's lived realities, rather there is a working reciprocity between the two. This work undertakes the task of determining how the story of Jesus is significant in evaluating the tenets of the #BlackLivesMatter movement.

#BlackLivesMatter is an ideological and political intervention sitting at the intersection of race, sex, gender, and religion, in a world where Black lives are systematically and intentionally targeted for death. The movement is an affirmation of Black contributions to this society, our humanity, and our resilience in the face of deadly oppression. Beyond a social media hash tag, it is connecting people across the country working to end the various intersecting forms of injustice impacting all of our people. It is creating space for the celebration and humanization of Black lives.[23] In other words, #BlackLivesMatter is a liberation movement.

The principal insight of liberation theology insists that redemption is not only the rescue of certain individuals for eternal life in another world, but the fulfillment of all humanity in the

21. Williams, *Sisters in the Wilderness*, 139.

22. Cone, *Said I Wasn't Gonna Tell Nobody*, 22.

23. BlackLivesMatter, "About Page."

political and social realities of this world.[24] Integral to the tenets of the #BlackLivesMatter movement is a spirituality of resistance, which implies that if an oppressed people have pride in their own culture and heritage, as well as a knowledge that they are children of God, then they will not be as vulnerable to the oppressive structures, systems, and ideologies that attempt to convince them that they are nobody, and that their lives are not worth living.[25] As oppressors band themselves together in order to keep the disinherited of the world in poverty, so the world's disinherited must enter into theo-political solidarity to create a movement of liberation.[26] Divisive and demoralizing behavior is made possible because a support base of religious folx are trafficking in a theo-logic that they rely on in order to enshrine in public policy to secure supremacy for themselves and their children for generations to come. There is a religiously based movement afoot with an impulse that is contrary to human flourishing rooted in an apocalyptic eschatology. To understand the religious ideology of a people is to know a lot about their politics, their social habits, their hopes and aspirations, their fears, their failures, and their understandings of who they are.[27] The underbelly of this movement is tied to themes of climate denial, white supremacy, anti-intellectualism, theocratic control of embodiment, and populism that verges on fascism.[28] The digital age has ushered in the opportunity for theology to emerge from the communities of the oppressed in real time across the global community and this particular movement is the fruit of the advances of technology.

In the wake of the trial of George Zimmerman for the killing of Trayvon Martin, #BlackLivesMatter was created by three Black queer women: Alicia Garza, Opal Tometi, and Patrisse Cullors.[29] These insightful women understood and responded to the reality

24. McFague, *Models of God*, 7.

25. Douglas, *Black Christ*, 106.

26. Gutierrez, *Theology of Liberation*, 12.

27. Frazier and Lincoln, *Negro Church in America*, 104.

28. Delay, *Against*, x.

29. Lightsey, *Our Lives Matter*, 66.

that in our society those who are judged as nonnormative or nonconforming do not merit inclusion into society's mainstream. Instead, they are ostracized, alienated, marginalized, and even punished both through legal and extralegal methods.[30] They further understood that conversations once engaged at Bible studies or other common spaces were now happening on phones via Facebook and other applications, allowing both instant access to information and instant feedback. Social media made it possible for young Black people to document interactions they believed to be injustices and expose others to their experiences.[31] The particularities of these women lend themselves to a conversation about the God claims of the movement they birthed.

The story of Jesus may indeed have profound significance to this movement when put into dialogue with the tenets of the movement. No society can arise or endure without some religious core or orientation; therefore, in its attempt to revitalize our society, it is imperative that the religious core of #BlackLivesMatter be well articulated.[32] Culture gives birth to religion and religion in turn gives us structures so that we can understand the presence of the holy. The event of Jesus is God's conscious decision to appear in a specific social location. The divine mind, will, and feelings selected the setting of poverty and marginalization for the birth of the one chosen to offer full humanity for all.[33] If culture comprises a people's total social heritage including language, ideas, habits, beliefs, customs, social organizations, and traditions, etc., then white culture built on white religion and theology certainly exists in the United States.[34] Jesus then comes to us in opposition of white theology by reason of his chosen social location on the underside of power. Not only the site of his birth and realities of his social location show God's alignment with those on the margins, his chosen associates and message of radical wealth redistribution

---

30. Douglas, *Sexuality and the Black Church*, 21.

31. Lowery, *They Can't Kill Us*, 15.

32. See Schweiker, "Public Theology," 123–38.

33. Hopkins, *Introducing Black Theology*, 25.

34. Douglas, *Sexuality and the Black Church*, 18.

give clear indication that the person and work of Jesus is a direct counter-narrative to the status quo. His message further allows us to see the divine mind as adversarial to a theology of dominance. The role of the church, which is the embodiment of the teachings of Jesus, is to become the place where the disparate parts of our humanity can be bound together and then kept from being separate again.[35] Theologizing the #BlackLivesMatter movement engages the whole of society in gospel values by focusing on the work of human wholeness, and it can serve as the site of prophetic critique of white culture, white religion, and white theology.

Black liberation theology, womanist theology, and queer theology are examples of the types of theological reflection that do the work of restoring the marginalized. They are specifically embodied theologies that empower people of these particular embodiments to speak about God in meaningful ways.They answer back to the white theology used to establish the infrastructures of dominance that marginalize people based on the perception of nonnormativity. In the latter half of the twentieth century a coalition formed between neoliberal capitalist interest, segregationist, and conservative Christians such that the desires merged into a new iteration of the faith.[36] The political production of this coalition emerged as a powerful force which backed candidates, got presidents elected, and provided the climate for the rise of the militarization of the police force. With rhetoric about being tough on crime this coalition supports the prison industrial complex and the new slavery of mass incarceration.

The #BlackLivesMatter movement offers an opportunity to direct the attention of the whole church to the descendants of the American slavocracy and call attention to theological answers to the practical situations of those on the margins. Biblical aspects of the community's faith-journey are revealed in sermons, songs, people's testimonies, liturgy, ritual, and in its socio-political-cultural affiliations in the world, such as #BlackLivesMatter.[37]

35. Spong, *New Christianity for a New World*, 168.
36. Delay, *Against*, 6.
37. Williams, *Sisters in the Wilderness*, 132.

Turning what has been a tool of oppression into a tool of deliverance is part of my ministry call. As a part of the Black experience, I acknowledge that imperialist, white-supremacist, capitalist, heteropatriarchy has devastated the Black community. The Black community holds in its DNA the trauma of the Maafa, the horrors of American apartheid, the psychological devastation of terror lynching, and the sickness of institutionalized and systemic racism. The American culture has formed an atmosphere of powerful and pervasive prejudgments—based on race, gender, sexuality, and religion—that comprises an active epistemic framework affecting what we see and how we engage the world around us.[38] This state of prolonged trauma is the climate that gave birth to the spirit of #BlackLivesMatter. Far too many Black people embody multiple sites of trauma, and Black embodiment and the experiences that come as a result of it is called intersectionality. Too often the concentration and effects of Black poverty offer a pretext for police incursions, arrests, and violence that fuel the antagonistic relationships between police and the Black community.[39] The truth is that most American institutions are rooted in anti-Blackness and the police are chief among those institutions. Anti-Black racism is any support of a racist policy through actions or inaction or expressing a racist idea. Racism is the marriage of racist policies and racist ideas that produce and normalize racial inequities.[40]

Historically, white liberal Christians understood integration to mean assimilation, and that meant Blacks rejecting their own culture by adopting European cultural values. The supposition that supported the white definition of integration was a belief that African cultural values were completely destroyed during slavery. If Blacks were to develop cultural self-knowledge, the thought was that they would find it by identifying with white American values.[41] The time is now for a theo-logic grounded in decolonization of the Black mind and redemption from the sins of the imperialist,

---

38. Kornegay, *Queering of Black Theology*, 6.

39. Taylor, *From #BlackLivesMatter to Black Liberation*, 113.

40. Kendi, *How to Be an Antiracist*, 20.

41. Gutierrez, *Theology of Liberation*, 63.

white-supremacist, heterosexist, capitalist, heteropatriarchy of the dominant culture.

This chapter represents the backbone of the foundation for this book, and provides a clarion quality control mechanism.[42] The theological parameters of the study are specific to heuristic constructive theology. While all liberation theology engages a hermeneutic of suspicion, this study also has a hermeneutic of hunger. A hermeneutic of suspicion begins by suspecting every text, every tradition, in terms of its legitimizing role in promoting the domination of the particular tradition. The hermeneutic of hunger suggests that the Bible is read as the answer to what oppression, illness, lack of education, and apathy inflict on human beings.[43] The experience of being oppressed by gender, race, or poverty does not limit the theology that emerges to women, people of color, or the poor. Rather, the particular experience of oppression(s) brings in to sharper focus what one asserts the heart of the gospel truly to be for one's own time.[44] All liberation theology belongs to a branch of religious thought that claims theology should be done from the purview of the poor and oppressed.[45]

#BLACKLIVESMATTER DEFINED AND THE MOVEMENT'S IMPLICIT THEOLOGY STREAMS

The theology streams prominent in the #BlackLivesMatter movement are Black liberation theology, womanist theology, and queer liberation theology. These are not explicit in the wording of the tenets of the movement, but a close look at the tenets reveal implicit God claims. The work of the theologian is often to hear the God claims embedded in a particular discourse. Like any other popular or social discourse the ear of the theologian is always attuned to what these movements have to say about the divine.

---

42. Sensing, *Qualitative Research*, 22.

43. Soelle, *Silent Cry*, 48.

44. McFague, *Models of God*, 47.

45. Perez, *Soulfully Gay*, 17.

The tenets of #BlackLivesMatter may appear to be anthropological and social, however just under the surface of the statements lies a rich invitation into a conversation about the divine.

Black Liberation Theology analyzes the condition of Blackness in light of God's revelation in Jesus Christ both to create a new understanding of Black dignity among Black people and to provide the necessary soul in that people to destroy racism.[46] Black theology recognizes that God, through Jesus Christ and the presence of the Holy Spirit, works with the poor as they learn to love themselves enough to practice their total freedom and create full humanity on earth as it is in heaven.[47] In the larger history of Christian theological reflection, Black Liberation theology has endeavored to give substance and systemic expression to a theological perspective that sees the work of salvation in the broadest of terms.[48] Built largely on the Hebrew scripture's narrative of the exodus and the Gospels' accounts of the person and work of Jesus, Black liberation theology establishes a theological foundation for the complete emancipation of Black people from white oppression by whatever means Black people deem necessary.[49] This work underscores the liberation theme as the central gospel message and the essential work of the church. Because #BlackLivesMatter is unapologetically Black, in that it affirms the collective value of Black embodiment, it is in and of itself a praxis of Black liberation theology. To love and desire freedom for Black people is the lens Black liberation theology seeks to contribute to the field of theological inquiry. Early Black liberation theologians needed to find a means to relate the Christian gospel to the Black experience in a way that did not condemn Black people's responses to their oppression. These early theologians were working to force theologians and the general body of the dominant culture to deal with Black people's particularities.[50]

46. Cone, *Black Theology and Black Power*, 117.

47. Hopkins, *Black Theology of Liberation*, 24.

48. Warnock, *Divided Mind of the Black Church*, 19.

49. Cone, *Black Theology and Black Power*, 6.

50. Douglas, *Black Christ*, 63.

An ethic of liberation arises out of love for ourselves and for humanity. This is the essential ingredient of liberation without which the struggle turns into a denial of what Divine liberation means.[51] For the Black liberation theologian, the fundamental act of God, the doing and ethics of God, is Divine liberation for all humanity. Earthly emancipation for those in bondage, both spiritual and material bondage, must operate in a co-constitutive fashion. The #BlackLivesMatter movement shares in Black liberation theology in that each sees the poor and broken-hearted as co-agents with Divine intention. This co-agency results in the full emancipation of Black bodies.

Since we cannot disregard Jesus as one who intentionally identified with those on the margins, the tenets of #BlackLivesMatter help us to identify more closely with Jesus the liberator. To be a Christian theologian is to seek, speak, and show understanding of what God was doing in Christ for the sake of the world.[52] The cross of Jesus, a paradoxical religious symbol, inverts the world's value system with the news that hope comes by way of defeat, that suffering and death do not have the last word, that the last shall be first and the first shall be last. A symbol of salvation in American culture, the cross is really an instrument of government-sanctioned execution. For Black people so familiar with the tools of murder used by the state the cross and the lynching tree are indissolubly linked. State-sanctioned murder is the history of Black bodies in America from the time of our kidnapping to today. The cross, the lynching tree, and the murder of Black people at the hands of police represent the worst in human beings and at the same time "an unquenchable ontological thirst" for life that refuses to let the worst determine our final meaning.[53] #BlackLivesMatter helps us make the theological and social move from the tragedy of the cross to the triumph of the resurrection.

51. Cone, *God of the Oppressed*, 217.
52. Vanhoozer and Strachan, *Pastor as Public Theologian*, 17.
53. Cone, *Cross and the Lynching Tree*, 3.

Womanist theology asks where God is in the lives of Black women and how Black women name God.[54] Contemporary womanist spirituality evolves from the nineteenth-century moral reform and woman's club movement. While it is a spirituality rooted in community, it is also concerned with the individual.[55] All theologizing that gives attention to Alice Walker's definition of womanism is considered womanist theology. Walker's definition includes being a Black feminist, as well as a woman who loves other women, sexually and/or non-sexually. In addition, a womanist is committed to the survival and wholeness of an entire people, male and female.[56] It must be clear that womanist theology is done by Black women for the larger collective. Men and others can offer work informed by womanist sensibilities, but must not attempt to appropriate womanism. The work of womanist scholars provides a theo-logic that is particular to the lived experiences of the Black women who have and continue to carve out this discipline. These theologies are a response to the exclusion of Black women's experience by classical feminism.[57] The value of feminist theory to Black women is diminished because it evolves from a white racial context that is seldom acknowledged.[58] The study and practice of womanist theology highly values Black women's epistemology (ways of knowing), rather than accepting them as peripheral to white feminist thought—it is not merely an addendum to a black version of feminism.[59] Womanist theology breaks from feminist theology in that it allows room for the wholeness of men as a core tenet, in this way it serves as a healing agency without divisiveness in the Black community. It would be impossible to separate #BlackLivesMatter from womanist theology; the Black women who founded the movement did so in response to the killing of a Black male. Womanist's concern for the wholeness of community

54. Mitchem, *Introducing Womanist Theology*, 46.
55. Townes, *Blaze of Glory*, 43.
56. Walker, *Search of Our Mother's Gardens*, xi.
57. Hopkins, *Black Theology of Liberation*, 129.
58. See Crenshaw, "Demarginalizing the Intersection," 139–68.
59. Smith, *Womanist Sass and Talk Back*, 30.

and acknowledgment that this concern be particular to the love of men is demonstrated by the response of the founders to place themselves on the frontlines of mass protests and demonstrations that grew out of the hashtag. Womanist theologians recognize that Eurocentric theology has been effectively much more about the control of women's bodies than about God; rather, discourse about God has focused on normalizing the white male embodiment and marginalizing all other forms of human ways of being in the world.[60] The tasks of womanist theology are to claim history; to declare the authority of Black women, men, and children; to learn from the experience of the forebears; to admit shortcomings and errors; and to improve the quality of women's lives.[61] A womanist theology engages a social-political analysis of wholeness and begins with a religio-cultural analysis. This analysis lifts up those aspects of Black life—that is, of Black religion and culture—that are sustaining and liberating for Black people. As it is bifocal, a sociopolitical analysis of wholeness will confront racism, sexism, classism, and heterosexism, not only as they impinge upon the Black community but also as they are nurtured within that community.[62] Thus, both internal and external pressure against the full humanity of Black women and Black bodies is explored through a womanist hermeneutic. In this way womanism helps the Black community unlearn the internal anti-Blackness that develops by the oppression of whiteness.

Because the #BlackLivesMatter movement has been founded by women and seeks to be an affirming space free from sexism, misogyny, and male-centeredness, a theological conversation must turn itself to the contribution of womanist theologians in these very areas. A womanist spirituality is a radical concern for is-ness in the context of African American life. This is-ness is physical and spiritual, and the #BlackLivesMatter movement attempts to speak to both the physical and spiritual embodiment of Black people. Is-ness marks the very nature of nature, of our breathing in and

60. See Beaudoin, "Postmodern Practical Theology," 194.
61. Lightsey, *Our Lives Matter*, 88.
62. Douglas, *Black Christ*, 99.

out as human beings, and the movement of creation itself. The ontological existence of Black people is under daily assault that often manifest in physical violence toward Black bodies. This constant trauma on the Black psyche necessitates salvific intervention. The primary concern then of the womanist theology embedded in the tenets of #BlackLivesMatter is concrete existence (lived life) and physic wellness, the impetus for a coherent and unified relationship between body, soul, and creation.[63] The womanist understanding says that a text cannot be understood apart from the world it creates in the imagination of the hearer. The effects of the text socially, emotionally, psychologically, and otherwise are vital to the extraction of meaning. Meaning has no productive existence outside its realization in the mind of the hearer; that is what produces faith.[64] Faith for Black women becomes a self-defining center that resists socially constructed stereotypes. The development of this faith is neither denial of social conditions nor a mere response to them. Rather, faith provides alternative space in which Black women become empowered. This faith becomes the grounding of the Black community, which these Black women ultimately nourish and which involves spiritual maturation for all.[65]

Womanist theology stands with Mary and the other women at the foot of the cross in faithful witness to the work of liberation. A theology of the people by the people, womanist theology is in conversation with Black liberation theology where privileging male otherness in Black liberation theology disregards the ontological implications of Black women's suffering.[66] The founding women of #BlackLivesMatter stand as witness—at the feet of murdered Black bodies—to the rumor of the resurrection of a whole community, and ultimately a nation. The story of Jesus informs this witness. We must pay closer attention to the ways in which Jesus was Immanuel and how we as partners with this witness must move into our own

63. Townes, *Blaze of Glory*, 48.
64. See Venable-Ridley, "Paul and African American Community" 212–33.
65. Mitchem, *Introducing Womanist Theology*, 49.
66. Terrell, *Power in the Blood*, 68.

ministries of faithfulness and hope.[67] It is this distinctive that moves the #BlackLivesMatter movement forward from past civil rights movements which failed to give voice to issues of gender equality. The womanist hermeneutic inherent in the #BlackLivesMatter movement is a distinctive and model for the healing of the Black community and particularly the Black Church.

Queer liberation theology, based on queer theory, is LG-BTQQIA+ people talking about God in a self-consciously transgressive manner, especially in terms of challenging societal norms about sexuality and gender. It challenges and deconstructs the natural binary categories of sexual and gender identity.[68] Queer theorist and subsequently queer theologians seek to examine the concept of "queer" in order to think about how society might construct identity that is truly liberating, transformative, and inclusive of all those who stand outside of the dominant constructed norm of state-sanctioned white middle- and upper-class heteropatriarchy.[69] This is the stream of theology that brings the sexualized discourse of #BlackLivesMatter into dialogue with the Black Church. Queer theology postulates that God gives gays and lesbians the rather startling variation of their sexuality to help their brothers and sisters have greater insights into the reality of their God.[70] While holding homosexuality as a Divine gift, queer theology is inclusive of this gift while not being limited to it. Queer theology is not a method of justifying behaviors and sexual acts, rather it is an enterprise focused on the wholeness of the person in relationship to themselves, others, and the divine.

Queering, as a theological methodology, is a deconstruction and re-evaluation of gender perspectives that uses as its framework queer theory; its resources are scripture, reason, tradition, and experience.[71] This identity-based liberation theology empowers LGBTQQIA+ people to develop modes of describing the

67. Townes, *Blaze of Glory*, 115.

68. Cheng, *Radical Love*, 9.

69. Johnson and Henderson, *Black Queer Studies*, 25.

70. Empereur, *Spiritual Direction and Gay Person*, 3.

71. Lightsey, *Our Lives Matter*, 27.

experiential consequences of these categories. To "queer" is to destabilize categories and transgress the idea of fixed identity, and as such queerness and queer theology are always developing. Queer theory and ultimately queer theology have at the center the impulse to disrupt any effort to reduce into simplistic dualism the experience of life or experience with the divine.[72] To give a definition of queer without understanding the fluidity of the term itself is to dishonor the intellectual tradition. At its best, Queer theology pursues the ending of discrimination against LGBTQQIA+ persons.[73] Queer theology is uncovering and celebrating the gifts that LGBTQQIA+ people bring to the church and the world and the ways in which Christianity has always been queer.[74] In this way #BlackLivesMatter comes into conversation with queerness not just through the sexuality of some Black people, rather because in our culture everything that comes into contact with Blackness is queered. The Black experience is a condition of queerness in which the "deployments of power" create a social construction of Black bodies.[75] Blackness like whiteness has a degree of fluidity (albeit to a much lesser extent). The lack of fixed character mixed with social disdain is quite destabilizing and transgressive—in a word, queer.

Since God has no material embodiment, it becomes important in queer theology that God is spirit. Spirit is life or intelligence conceived of entirely apart from physical embodiment. It is vital essence, force, energy, as distinct from matter.[76] Queer theology says that God is beyond gender and yet present in every point of the gender continuum. This God force or allness is manifested in human genders in all the beautiful arrays of gender identities that manifest themselves, in that all humans are created in the *imago Dei*. Gender then refers to all the manifestations of masculinity or femininity that are not immediately, demonstrably biological.

---

72. Edman, *Queer Virtue*, 3.

73. Lightsey, *Our Lives Matter*, 77.

74. Queer Theology, "Home Page."

75. Kornegay, *Queering of Black Theology*, 99–100.

76. Holmes, *Science of Mind*, 81.

These include conventions of dress, mannerisms, social roles, speech patterns, and much more. Gender refers to the cultural meanings that overwrite the physical body.[77] For the purposes of the work of queer theology, we have biological sex inherently present in our bodies, but we *do* gender; it is performative.[78]

Two of the main tenets of #BlackLivesMatter address the LGBTQQIA+ community specifically; hence, any study of the movement in conversation with theology would be diminished and inadequate without a serious consideration of queer theology. There is a long history of African bodies as subjects of attack and denigration by Western and also Eastern culture, as well as black bodies being viewed as exotic mysteries, cursed mutations, and the lowest of the Western world's bodily caste system.[79] #BlackLivesMatter's core tenets speak to this history and the particular ways that the range of the Black sexual spectrum must be acknowledged. While the life and work of Jesus did not focus on same-gender-loving people, Jesus does stop to address the issue of gender-nonconforming people in Matt 19 during a discourse on marriage. This ethic continues in Acts 8:26–39 with the conversion of the Ethiopian eunuch. Here Phillip leads this gender nonconforming person of color to conversion, but never in any way addresses the sexuality of the situation; this is considered by many scholars the first gentile conversion.[80] #BlackLivesMatter continues the trajectory of this witness by intentionally lifting queer and transgender people up to be affirmed as members of the beloved community. From the first gatherings in Ferguson, Missouri, Black queer clergy were present in the movement. Queer clergy and extremely conservative clergy joined arm in arm in the Ferguson protest by intentionally bringing their theological locations with them and yet holding them gently enough to get the work done.[81]

77. Buechel, *That We Might Become God*, 7.

78. Blank, *Straight*, 11.

79. Lightsey, *Our Lives Matter*, 33.

80. Weekly, *Homosexianity*, 113.

81. Francis, *Ferguson and Faith*, 4.

Because #BlackLivesMatter sits at the intersection of race, sex, gender, and religion, its God claims are intersectional as well. It moves Black liberation theology forward into queer liberation theology through the door of womanist theology. Queering, as a theological methodology, is a deconstruction and re-evaluation of gender perspectives that uses as its framework queer theory.[82] This queering of Black liberation theology is necessary because Black theology heretofore has limited liberation to those Black bodies that fulfill heteronormative hegemonic masculinity tropes.[83] #BlackLivesMatter is a theological challenge to the unwritten contract between Black liberation theology, Black patriarchy, and the Black Church in that it does not by its tenets affirm a reifying of middle-class white heteropatriarchal norms.

SUMMARY

This chapter outlined the need to find theological language to support the action of #BlackLivesMatter. As delineated above, the conversation relies on the work of James Cone, Pamela Lightsey, Stephanie Mitchem, Cornel West, and Kelly Brown Douglas to develop the Black liberation, queer, and womanist theologies that ground the contribution this book makes to sustain the #BlackLivesMatter movement. It is important here to lift up this Black scholarship, as Black scholars are often robbed of credit and acknowledgment. These fine scholars sit in opposition to the narrative that theology must be done in conversation with the scholarship of the dominant culture. The particular lens through which these scholars offer their insights are beneficial to the universal realities of humanity, because they are not afraid of their own particulars and are willing to give theological attention to them. The next chapter considers the methodology developed in response to, and support of, the research question and purpose.

82. Lightsey, *Our Lives Matter*, 27.
83. Kornegay, *Queering of Black Theology*, 4–5.

CHAPTER 3

METHODOLOGY

INTRODUCTION

THE THEOLOGICAL DISCUSSION OF the #BlackLivesMatter movement is far too important to be left to one person's understanding.
This chapter offers an overview relative to the purpose and process
of my research, as well as the specific research questions covered.
Both my background and role as researcher will be discussed, as
well as the limitations and delimitations of this qualitative research
study. The chapter defines relevant key terms, identifies the plan
for conducting research, and also looks at the theological questions to be examined. Finally, the chapter assesses relevant ethical
issues related to the research and then concludes with a summary.

OVERVIEW OF PURPOSE AND RESEARCH
QUESTIONS

Tim Sensing, a leading expert in research methodologies, reminds
us that conversations of this nature are intended to serve the
church, develop ministerial practice, and be applicable to other
practitioners in the field.[1] He further contends that qualitative

1. Sensing, *Qualitative Research*, xv.

methodology allows us to draw the human and theoretical elements of practical theology into conversation for the advancement of the field and the church. This type of research ensures that the thesis will be both public and usable, offering professional contributions in keeping with high standards of productive theological research.[2]

The primary purpose of this basic qualitative research study is to explore the intersections among womanist, Black liberation, and queer liberation theologies within the #BlackLivesMatter movement in the US. Secondarily, the study hopes to discover how these theologies impact the way Black Church clergy can engage the movement in actionable ways. The particulars of the movement's founders lend themselves very easily to these theological lenses, and the movement that has grown is intentionally inclusive of those who reflect the realities that bring these theological streams together.

METHODS

First, I addressed written surveys to four academically trained and practical theologians.[3] These activist-scholars are all active in the #BlackLivesMatter movement and in other justice movements specific to their theological specialty. It is important to hear from the academy for its theological vocabulary and it is equally important to hear from practical theologians because they can provide the language of the commons. The theologians queried come from Trinity College in Hartford, Connecticut, the American Baptist Seminary of the West in Berkeley, California, and two national nonprofit organizations connected to the work of #BlackLivesMatter. The two nonprofits focus on LGBTQ understanding in the Black Church context and womanist and LGBTQ theology in conversation with the United Church of Christ. These theologians were chosen based on the recognition they have earned in their particular fields as well as their activity

2. Sensing, *Qualitative Research*, 59.

3. Patton, *Qualitative Research and Evaluation*, 4.

in the #BlackLivesMatter movement. The questions asked are the six questions that have driven my interest in the theology of #BlackLivesMatter. And, just as importantly, they are questions that have arisen in the life of my local congregation.

- What do you see as the primary God claims in the #Black-LivesMatter movement?

- How does the praxis of #BlackLivesMatter reveal its theology?

- How can #BlackLivesMatter reconcile womanist, Black liberation, and queer theologies?

- What theological needs in the Black community and larger Christian communion does the #BlackLivesMatter movement address?

- What does it mean to be a theologian whose place for doing theology is within the #BlackLivesMatter movement?

- What should the church's response to the #BlackLivesMatter movement be?

With a set of questions reflecting the tenets of the #BlackLivesMatter movement, our survey of Black, academically trained theologians in Black liberation, womanist, and queer liberation theologies begins to uncover the theological underpinnings of the movement itself.[4] Following the written query of the theologians and after coding for themes, I tested the findings in a focus group. The coding places the raw data into logical, meaningful categories, so the data can be examined in a holistic fashion. By placing the data into meaningful categories, I am better able to communicate the interpretation in useful ways for the academy, the church, and the #BlackLivesMatter movement.[5] The coded findings provides a rubric for a theological discussion that will ultimately put the #BlackLivesMatter movement in dialogue with the whole Christian communion. Modern scholars must serve modern movements in the same way that Rev. Dr. King

4. Patton, *Qualitative Research and Evaluation*, 4.
5. Sensing, *Qualitative Research*, 194.

and Rev. Thurman provided a robust theological framework for the civil rights movement—a framework that expanded during the span of the movement. Movements are not static; they are always developing—likewise, the theological discussion within the movement. I am in this book attempting to identify the theo-logic that gives the movement its shape and character.

During coding ten themes emerged; I choose seven to present to my focus group because these seven showed up equally in all the responses to the survey. These surveys, which were structured to provide the theologians with open-ended questions, were administered via email in April of 2016, and all responses were returned by May 2016. The coding was completed between May and June in time for the June focus group in Lombard, Illinois. At the conclusion of the surveying and coding process, I convened a focus group of twenty pastoral leaders from across the country to ascertain the viability of the interviews.[6] The focus group was made up of pastoral leaders who were actively serving African American congregations across the country. In the group were four women and sixteen men. Four people present in the room were not pastors; their input was not included in the study. The pastors represented congregations from each geographic region of the country and represented Baptist, Pentecostal, nondenominational, Methodist, and United Church of Christ congregations.

The pastors questioned ranged in age from early thirties to early seventies. There was one set of co-pastors who share senior pastor duties, and two associate pastors present. Pastors participating were among those who meet annually at the Love Fellowship Music and Arts Conference. They sign up to participate in sessions each day. This focus group was one of the sessions they chose to attend. Upon entering the room, everyone was informed about the purpose of the focus group; no one opted out. The focus group was presented with the tenets of the #BlackLivesMatter movement and the theological themes that surfaced as a result of the surveys. Appendix B contains the PowerPoint presentation slides that were verbally and visually presented at the beginning of the focus group

6. Sensing, *Qualitative Research*, 120.

session; these slides prompted the recorded discussion. Notes were made based on the recording to assure anonymity. There are many other demographic identifiers that were left unstated to maintain the participants' anonymity. I verbally presented the PowerPoint slides to ensure that all the material was covered equally. I was available to clarify any questions regarding definitions or other information. The slides were shown so that more visual learners could digest the material.

As noted previously, the focus group was convened to determine the response of Black pastors to the theologians' themes. After the focus group met, the findings were reviewed and coded. The findings were placed with the codes that they represented to determine the viability of #BlackLivesMatter in the life of the Black Church.[7]

I considered, as I began to develop my approach to this research area, that my subject is a living, ongoing movement. My attempt was to situate and explain this living movement through the lens of both established older theologies and emerging newer theologies. The #BlackLivesMatter movement was established in 2013 in response to Trayvon Martin's murder; hence, it is so new and rapidly changing that any research may quickly become outdated.[8] In the presentation of my research, I also considered my first audience and their familiarity with the movement and the theological traditions I intended to engage.

The challenge that most captured my attention was maintaining the posture of researcher. I am passionate about the topic and have built many relationships within the #BlackLivesMatter movement. While friendship with those interviewed may foster openness, it also creates some level of risk.[9] The participants may assume that my assessment of the movement's theological claims is generally the overall community voice. While a concern at the beginning of the project, this did not bear true throughout the process, as I was pleased to discover.

7. Patton, *Qualitative Research and Evaluation*, 496.

8. Garza, "Herstory of #BlackLivesMatter Movement," lines 1–3.

9. Sensing, *Qualitative Research*, 21.

Undertaking this particular project also risks inducing strong reactions from my national church—and my local congregation!—with regard to seeing the #BlackLivesMatter movement through a liberative lens. It is my understanding that many times congregations feel disconnected from their pastor when the pastor seeks to engage works of public theology; thus defeating the purpose of doing work that is designed to foster ministerial depth in the local congregation.[10] My local congregation, however, has been a source of support and celebration throughout the entirety of the project.

BACKGROUND AND ROLE OF RESEARCHER

As a Black male academician who is actively pastoring a predominantly Black local congregation *and* serving as Bishop of Operations for a predominantly Black Reformation, the #BlackLivesMatter movement is of great relevance for me and the people I serve. My role as pastor includes the charge to provide congregants with the theological and spiritual tools to navigate the particularities and intersectionality of their human experience. As a pastor and bishop, I see the church as that people called into being by the power and love of God to share in God's revolutionary activity for the liberation of humanity.[11] The church is to me a community of people bound together by their willingness to journey into meaning.

As pastor and bishop my job is to partner with parishioners and leaders alike on that very particular journey.[12] It is my task and privilege to assist congregants in making theological sense out of the rash of killings that have gone on for decades, but now are being publicized, video-taped, and exposed in ways never before experienced. This allows the community to say what the community can do and is doing. In addition, I currently serve on

10. Sensing, *Qualitative Research*, xxxiii.

11. Cone, *Black Theology and Black Power*, 63.

12. Spong, *New Christianity*, 238.

the King County Juvenile Disproportionality Steering Committee, which is giving eighteen months of our time to police/community relations. This civic engagement is in keeping with the prophetic tradition and vocation of the Black Church. Prophetic traditions aim to transform the world in God's name and see authentic religious experience as a world-shaping force.[13] This is the historical faith tradition that informs and shapes my call and scholarship. All of this situates me as a researcher who is deeply connected to his research. In all of this work my personal goal is to allow the voices from the margins to have the language and the platform to speak truth to power.

LIMITATIONS AND DELIMITATIONS

While the #BlackLivesMatter movement has in some cases reached international status, this study examines, in a US context, the realities that gave rise to the movement. I focus on Black theologians active in the movement, as it is of the utmost importance that the movement itself be responsible for codifying its theology. The events dating from the Ferguson shooting of Michael Brown to through the end of President Barack H. Obama's administration in January of 2017 provide the historical context of this particular research project. It is important that the study moves from Ferguson and not from the death of Trayvon Martin, when the hashtag first appeared, in that what began in Ferguson as a local struggle of ordinary Black people grew, in one hundred days, into a national movement against police brutality and daily killings of unarmed Black citizens.[14] The events of St. Louis and the widespread police brutality against Black embodiment stand in the light of the administration of the first US president who shares Black identity. Just as the period following the Civil War and Reconstruction generated white resistance in the form of Jim and Jane Crow, married to lynching across the country, so

13. Volf, *Public Faith*, 7.

14. Taylor, *From #BlackLivesMatter to Black Liberation*, 2.

the political advancement of the Black race to the presidency has been met with the current attack on Black embodiment. Whether at the hands of the police or ordinary citizens, the murder and subsequent media frenzy related to the mutilation of Black bodies during the first Black presidency has been staggering.

While the socio-religious narrative of the Black community has been to posit our leaders in the deliverer motif of Moses, the presidency of Barak Obama has brought very little deliverance to Black lives. From Michael Dunn, who killed unarmed Jordan Davis, to Dylan Roof, who massacred nine Black people in a church while attending a Bible study with them, there is a predictable resurgence of white terror that has accompanied our first Black presidency. While the Black president himself has often upheld an extremely optimistic view of racial progress, Ferguson is not a singular situation. It is an object lesson in the national policing practices that have created the largest incarcerated population in the Western world, as well as a veil of permanent racial suspicion.[15]

From the aftermath of slavery forward, Black scholars have understood that Black people cannot rely on the culture that subjugated, exploited, and oppressed Black people to interpret Black reality.[16]

15. Dyson, *Black Presidency*, 31.
16. hooks, *Rock My Soul*, 96.

CHAPTER 4

PROJECT FINDINGS

BLACK CHURCH EXPERIENCE SURVEY

THIS PROJECT COMMENCED WITH an introduction of the research, the research question, context, framework, and methodology. A theological reflection situated the work in the larger theological conversation of justice and liberation. This reflection helped to inform the sociopolitical question about what pastors might do as a result of understanding the God claims of the #BlackLivesMatter movement. After contextualizing the project with theological insight, the next step required a methodology that would hone the research questions and shape the research.

To understand a broad cross-section of the Black Church experience, those who were identified as leaders in the church and also engaged in the #BlackLivesMatter movement were queried, via a survey, about the theological assumptions of the movement. The original survey data was collected and, within the compiled responses, key words and ideas were noted; from these, codes were perceived and highlighted. From these codes seven unanimous themes emerged. An appropriate research method evolved from this process and a focus group format was chosen since the research involved the responses of pastors to understanding the theological claims of a social phenomenon. Subsequently, a focus group of twenty pastors was convened. These pastors actively serve African American congregations across the country; they meet annually at the Love Fellowship Music and Arts Conference. Attendees sign up to participate in sessions each day. This focus group was presented as one of the sessions they opted to attend.

It became evident that the theologians agree that the #BlackLivesMatter movement is one that stands for equality and justice while evoking the claim of *imago Dei*. The focus of this movement is intersectionality and reconciling all of Black lived experience—specifically targeting the most marginalized and disenfranchised of the community. #BlackLivesMatter calls on leaders who are willing to embrace the risks associated with prophetic praxis and activism. After coding survey responses, I researched each theme to contextualize it for presentation to the focus group. These short statements represent the research of the seven unanimous themes that emerged from my analysis and coding of the surveys. Once the coded themes were explained, the results from the surveys were presented using the direct voices of the interviewees. Finally, this work presents the focus group results in the voices of the participants. First, however, the seven major themes are briefly discussed.

EQUALITY AND JUSTICE

Justice and equality address the systemic provision for the distribution of goods, as well as the burdens, of a society. Addressing societal violations also falls into the realm of equality and justice. Justice overarches legal right. It also condemns a legality that undermines fellowship or one that fails to listen to the intrinsic claim to dignity and well-being that all humans possess.[1] There are four faces of justice: distributive, contributive, commutative, and retributive.[2] #BlackLivesMatter is a movement that speaks to all

1. Farley, *Tragic Vision and Divine Compassion*, 82.
2. Heagle, *Justice Rising*, 52.

aspects of justice and the socioreligious implications of justice are clearly seen in its tenets. Equality has as its primary consideration rendering unto each person their due and balancing the interest and claims of individuals and groups as to decenter any sense of privilege or marginalization.

IMAGO DEI

Imago Dei is the theological concept (based on Gen 1:26–34) that God made the first people in a way that very much resembles God's own self. The doctrine purports that humanity is made in God's image and, therefore, individuals are of sacred worth.[3] Further, the doctrine of *imago Dei* postulates that humanity in its authenticity is united with God in character and nature—even if brokenness and sin, in some theologies, has transgressed this original nature.[4] In light of this, our task—as people made in the image and likeness of God—is to overcome the temptation not to love and appreciate all those whom God has called *good*.[5] In light of the history of Jesus Christ we often interpret *imago Dei* as an *imago Christi*. As the incarnation happens in utmost solidarity with and on behalf of the poor, so then the imprint of the divine is always present in those on the margins.[6]

INTERSECTIONALITY

Intersectionality addresses the combination of individuals' multiple social groups and the identification, experiences, and worldviews that result from this combination.[7] In particular terms, intersectionality defines the ways in which the most disinherited of the marginalized experience their lived reality in the face

3. Lightsey, *Our Lives Matter*, 79.

4. Ruether, *Sexism and God Talk*, 93.

5. Lightsey, *Our Lives Matter*, 81.

6. Migliore, *Faith Seeking Understanding*, 145.

7. Yarber and Sanders, *Microaggressions in Ministry*, 159.

of imperialist, white-supremacist, capitalist, heteropatriarchy. Intersectionality highlights the way one's race, class, gender, and sexuality (and the multiple combinations thereof) posture you in relationship to power and privilege.[8] A poor immigrant Black African lesbian woman experiences the effects of intersectionality in ways that a white heterosexual male member of the wealthy class never will. The reality—i.e., interlocking political systems that are foundational to our nation's politics—serves to create an extreme underclass. Most historical conversations of marginalization have centered singular identity politics, they overlook the convergence of multiple prejudices on subjects living at the intersections of racial, gender, sexual, and economic marginalization.[9]

RECONCILING THE WHOLE BLACK EXPERIENCE AND INCLUSION

African Americans have spent their years of freedom seeking (1) to gain respectability from the dominant culture as sexually moral beings, and (2) to overcome the historical labeling as a sexually perverse people.[10] To that end there has been both heteropatriarchy and homophobia within the community that has further marginalized those people within an already marginalized and disenfranchised group. Because the insular, privatized nuclear family is upheld as a model of Western family stability, all other forms—for example, the extended family, the female-headed family, the lesbian family—are devalued.[11] This has left many within the Black community feeling as if no place of belonging exists for them. Governmental agencies have contributed to the continued marginalization of non-heteropatriarchy in Black communities through bias reports such as the Moynihan Report which produced in the public discourse the notion of the Black

8. Johnson and Henderson, *Black Queer Studies*, 45.

9. Mumford, *Not Straight, Not White*, 5.

10. Griffin, *Their Own Received Them Not*, 20.

11. See Clarke, "Failure to Transform," 190–201.

"Welfare Queen." This report also fed the notion that the majority of underclass young Black men engage in reckless heterosexual behavior, becoming irresponsible baby factories.[12] Moynihan constructed an image of the Black male as an adolescent delinquent hustler, permanently emasculated by segregation and dominant Black women.[13] This pathologizing of the Black experience has become pervasive in American culture.

MARGINALIZATION AND DISENFRANCHISEMENT

Marginalization refers to those people who lack social status and live at the edges of or between the cracks of society. They are not a part of what is considered the mainstream or dominant culture. Often marginality means being economically poor and living in underdeveloped circumstances.[14] Marginalization is the result of the overarching system of Powers that are characterized by oppressive political relations, biased race relations, patriarchal gender relations, unjust economic relations, and the use of violence of various forms to maintain them all.[15] Disenfranchisement on the other hand speaks specifically to the denial of full democratic rights to people based on race or other identity politics.[16] This shows up as denying the full humanity of Black people, as promised in the Constitution, or as denying the right to vote to convicted felons in the time of mass incarceration in the prison industrial complex. This practice is woven into the fabric of American society and goes back the conquest of North American lands from Indigenous peoples. It found its strongest support in a theo-logic known as the Doctrine of Conquest, when the Borgia Pope gave Spain the

12. Johnson and Henderson, *Black Queer Studies*, 40–41.

13. Mumford, *Not Straight, Not White*, 53.

14. Empereur, *Spiritual Direction and the Gay Person*, 52.

15. Wink, *Powers That Be*, 39.

16. Manning, *Living Black History*, 115.

right to concur all lands that were not Catholic and thereby also controlled by Europeans.[17]

PROPHETIC PRAXIS AND ACTIVISM

Prophetic praxis is behavior that engages counter-cultural practices on behalf of the least among us.[18] For the church this praxis is rooted in the teaching of Jesus and an understanding of Jesus' preference for the poor. For the otherwise spiritual and nonreligious this is based in the pursuit of justice. Activism can be defined as organized and organic forms of resistance. That is, resistance is defined as the physical, overt expression of an inner attitude.[19] Critiquing racism alone is not activism. Activism has power and policy change as its primary objective and outcome.[20] Advocacy that is outcome-based and moves from changing minds and attitudes to changing policy is activism.

WILLINGNESS TO RISK AS LEADERS

In the current cultural climate, taking on the risks of leadership is extremely complicated. Clearly defined hierarchical structures are giving way to more horizontal infrastructures that offer greater flexibility, room for initiative, and the corresponding uncertainties that accompany these shifts.[21] Leaders with positions of high rank or title are no longer guaranteed followers.[22] Present social ethics, at least those espoused within the #BlackLivesMatter movement, indicate leadership must be earned through transparent relationship; leadership is no longer bestowed or conferred by reason of position. The social contract of this era means that

17. Hill Fletcher, *Sin of White Supremacy*, 6–7.
18. Marsh, *Beloved Community*, 144.
19. Turman, "Conversation with Dr. Turman."
20. Kendi, *How to Be an Antiracist*, 209.
21. Heifetz and Linsky, *Leadership on the Line*, 4.
22. McNeal, *Work of Heart*.

leadership is earned by relationship and experience over time. Any stance or position on any topic places the leader at risk of diminished capacity to lead or conversely may increase that leader's capacity to lead.

Once the focus group was armed with both the key themes from the surveys, coupled with the clear definitions I provided, it began its conversation about the themes. Subsequent to the focus group gathering in Lombard, Illinois, I coded the focus group findings to determine conclusions. The Black Church, like the communities it represents, is not a monolith. Just as there are multiple ways of constructing Blackness, there are multiple ways of being the Black Church.[23] To capture a wide snapshot of the Black Church, the focus group held at the Love Fellowship Music and Arts Seminar pastor's session included liberal, conservative, small church, large church, queer- and straight-identified, male, and female pastors.

For this book the presentation of results is broken up into two sections. The first presents the findings of the survey; the second the findings of the focus group. The following reflections are an interpretive review based on the context of the themes. Before offering concluding thoughts for this chapter, the significance and applicability of the study are noted.[24]

SURVEY FINDINGS

The theologians surveyed agreed that the #BlackLivesMatter movement is focused on equality and justice as it pertains to the law and those empowered to enforce the law. Because Black bodies, Black people, and Black lives, live under the constant constraints of white-supremacist thinking and systems of domination, the #BlackLivesMatter movement has emerged as an agent of resistance for all people who seek justice. Imperative to the idea of equality and justice is the inclusion of all Black lives, with special

---

23. Touré, *Who's Afraid of Post Blackness*, 149.
24. Sensing, *Qualitative Research*, 216.

attention being paid to the most marginalized of the marginalized: women and LGBTQQIA+ members of the community.

From the sixteenth century forward, European male travelers fabricated reports that made Black sexuality an icon for deviant sexuality in general.[25] In that way all Black sexuality is queer, when positioned over against white patriarchal heteronormativity. For people who find themselves on the margins, operating through multiple identities and unrecognized, traditional, single identity-based politics, theoretical conceptualizations of queerness hold great political promise.[26] All the theologians offered some explanation of current injustice based on the American value gap—that is, no matter our stated principles or how much progress we think we have made, white people are valued more than others in this country.[27] The cry of #BlackLivesMatter, according to the theologians surveyed, is a direct response to the global value gap and offers an alternative narrative for a better future.

The theologians surveyed were clear that the tenets of #BlackLivesMatter are centered in the *imago Dei*, which requires us to recognize and honor one another as humans who are beloved of God. No diminution of personhood based on ethnicity, sexuality, gender, or class should in any way be tolerated. The #BlackLivesMatter movement calls society into awareness of the ways in which, collectively, our society fails to live into honoring *imago Dei*. In the created order, no individual or group can be given right of privilege that allows them to "other" another; no racial construct or premise for marginalization is valid. Black communities are desperately in need of a faith-based message addressing the sacred identity of the Black body.

The theologians agreed that the tenets of the #BlackLivesMatter movement attempt to address fully the nuances of the Black experience. The movement, in its stated core values, is intentionally holistic. The voices of women, the transgendered, and youth are all centered in the tenets of #BlackLivesMatter, and intersectional

25. Copeland, *Enfleshing Freedom*, 12.

26. Johnson and Henderson, *Black Queer Studies*, 24.

27. Glaude, *Democracy in Black*, 31.

injustices are met head on. By centering the brilliance, experience, and leadership of women and the unique particularities of Black women, #BlackLivesMatter addresses the intersectional realities that the civil rights movement failed to address. As far back as the early movement against lynching in the United States, women have been instrumental in the struggle against white supremacy. However, the way in which #BlackLivesMatter has been intentional about keeping woman's issues tied to racial uplift, and the centering of women in power in public ways, is unique to the identity of the movement. During the anti-lynching movement, men like W. E. B. Du Bois and James Weldon Johnson were more public in their leadership roles. Women were far more active at the grass roots level in churches, the NAACP, and other male-led organizations. #BlackLivesMatter seems to flip on its head the paradigm long associated with Black justice movements.

Theologians spoke about #BlackLivesMatter as a movement to bring together the whole of the Black experience across the spectrum of identities. In the decades since the civil rights movement there has been what some would call a serious rupture or fragmenting of the Black community. Ethnic diversity undermines any easy idea of Black America. Between 1960 and 1984, more than 600,000 immigrants—from places like Jamaica and Trinidad—made their way to the United States. They were joined by more than 140,000 Haitian immigrants.[28] To speak of the Black community is both to speak of the collective group of Black people alive today and the set of institutions that have traditionally served as the foundations of Black communities. #BlackLivesMatter is the opportunity to connect the disparate parts of the Black experience in the common goal of justice. While race prejudice remains in America, there no longer seems to be a sense of race-brotherhood in the same sense that once defined the struggle for civil rights. So long as the best elements of a community do not feel duty-bound to protect and train and care for the weaker members of their group, they leave them to be preyed upon.[29]

28. Glaude, *Democracy In Black*, 123.
29. DuBois, *Souls of Black Folk*, 129.

#BlackLivesMatter is perfectly positioned to produce a theology that reaches to the most distanced of marginalized people(s). The theologians lifted the idea that #BlackLivesMatter offers a remedy and answer for both white fear and white rage. White fear is the general frame of mind that Black people are dangerous—because they are prone to criminal behavior—not only to white individuals, but to the overall well-being of our society.[30] White rage is triggered inevitably by Black advancement. It is not the mere presence of Black people that is the problem; rather it is Blackness with ambition, with drive, with purpose, with aspirations, and with demands for full and equal citizenship.[31] The problem of race in America has always been a problem of power. White supremacy is the legacy of power not ignorance regarding the sacredness of Blackness. The surveyed theologians point to #BlackLivesMatter as a movement that decenters whiteness by holding up the value of Blackness. Bell hooks often uses the phrase "imperialist white-supremacist capitalist patriarchy" to describe the interlocking political systems that are the foundation of our nation's politics; the tenets of #BlackLivesMatter systematically undermine each of the constructs that have created the American caste system.[32]

The theologians noted the need for the church to embrace the prophetic tradition of speaking truth to power as directed by a God who demands justice; likewise, the church must embody Jesus' instruction to take up the cross and follow Him. That Jesus bodily committed acts of resistance against empire and systems of domination cannot be lost on the church as a part of the analysis of #BlackLivesMatter. Racism is a moral catastrophe, most graphically seen in the prison-industrial complex and the targeted police surveillance in Black and Brown ghettos that is rendered invisible in public discourse.[33] It is not lost on the theologian's gaze that #BlackLivesMatter is in the same tradition of historical resistance

30. Glaude, *Democracy In Black*, 74.

31. Anderson, *White Rage*, 4.

32. hooks, *Will to Change*, 17.

33. King, *Radical King*, xi.

movements where marching to bring awareness to a moral and spiritual failure is a major component. This moral appeal must never be mistaken for a conversation of morality void of understanding the dynamics of power, for moral suasion void of power has been the downfall of progressivism.

A major theme that the theologians recognized was that #BlackLivesMatter includes a call to action on the part of leaders. Jesus' awareness of his ministry charge, noted in Luke 4:18, was in the prophetic tradition of Isaiah; therefore, if leaders are to be faithful to the work of Jesus they will engage prophetic praxis. Freedom is acquired by conquest, not by gift.[34] This engagement will always cause leaders to risk popularity and possibly even safety. Such vulnerability for them includes the task of critical theological reflection; this should result in leaders who think critically about the role of family formation in their own history, their ecclesial formation, and their social context. The willingness on the part of leaders to risk is based to some degree on the decolonization of the mind of the leaders. All this is needed to be faithful to gospel values as seen in the person and work of Jesus.[35]

FOCUS GROUP RESPONSES

The Focus group was convened and presented the findings of the theologians' surveys via PowerPoint presentation (Appendix B). While fully agreeing with the sentiments of #BlackLivesMatter as a response to the value gap, the majority of pastors in the focus group rejected the assertion that equality and justice had a responsibility to include the most marginalized. They chose to classify sexuality as a matter of choice and therefore a matter of sin. Powerfully, they argued that the task of the church should be calling sinners to repentance and that efforts to stand in solidarity with the LGBTQ community for rights was a betrayal of the message of the Bible for true moral living. Only a few of the pastors stood in support of the

---

34. Freire, *Pedagogy of Freedom*, 47.
35. Francis, *Ferguson and Faith*, 37.

overall God claims of the movement as the tenets point to equality for those most disenfranchised within the Black experience. One represented church reported that about 50 percent of the congregation is now same-gender loving. That local assembly does not preach against equality, but also does not allow openly LGBTQ people to hold leadership positions. This unwritten and unspoken policy gives voice to the tension in local churches about where the Black Church stands on issues of equality and justice. The pastors do not see social justice as inclusive of sexuality because they cannot conceptualize explicit recognition of the relationship between racial and sexual oppression.

I found that the pastors of the focus group lived into the traditional narrative around heterosupremacy that has long been attached to the Black Church. To overcome historical labeling as a sexually perverse people, Black people have spent their time, post-legalized slavery, seeking to be seen by mainstream society as sexually moral beings. In an effort to receive acceptance from a homophobic society, Blacks strongly condemn and even deny homosexuality both within the Black community and Black churches.[36] Heterosupremacy does not always mean a hatred of gay persons, but it is always the centering and avocation of heterosexism.[37] The pastors in the focus group spoke in a manner that called for the special rights of heterosexual people only, such as legally sanctioned marriages, which is the very definition of heterosexism.

The focus group mostly agreed with *imago Dei* as a fundamental building block of the church. They even identified *imago Dei* as core to Black liberation theology; however, several of the pastors indicated that evangelical fundamentalism and its core tenets were of greater import in their Black congregations than Black liberation theology. That we are all made in God's image was not debatable, but the doctrine of original sin informs the need to be born again. Anything that could be classified as sin, which for many includes homosexuality or transgenderism, necessitates rebirth. Those who claim these sins to be a part of their identity

36. Griffin, *Their Own Received Them Not*, 20.
37. Perez, *Soulfully Gay*, 39.

have a breach in revealing the character and nature of God. The tension lies between what constitutes a behavior and what is one's God-given nature.

To the majority of the pastors, sexuality is a behavior. I found that the focus group bore witness to the type of Christian hypocrisy that has long been critiqued in the church. In describing their ethical commitments, Christians sometimes claim to believe in the intrinsic moral worth of all human persons, but at the same time insistently support practices of discrimination against persons whose sexual identity does not carry the societal label of "heterosexual."[38] After the discussion on cis-gender male privilege, one pastor stated emphatically there are only two genders and they are male and female. These genders are identifiable by genitalia and there is never any confusion. Without a pause to consider that the oversimplification of subject does damage to the fullness of the subject, the pastors dismissed any possibility that a larger conversation be convened with regard to sexually minoritized people within the church.

The pastors had no pushback around intersectionality. They shared openly and freely about lived realities of their congregants and the complexities of the systems they are forced to engage. Women make up much of the church, and it is obvious that this movement differs from the civil rights movement in that women, for the most part, were not given prominent public leadership roles in that movement. The topic of congregations trying to redefine the role of women in the church was a major conversation among the pastors. The women pastors had much to say in this area as they found a place of solidarity with the founders of the #BlackLivesMatter movement. All of the gathered pastors agreed that equality for women is fundamental and that women must hold equal place in institutional leadership; however, just beneath the surface of that sentiment is the reality that everyone is still trying to figure out what that praxis will be. There seemed to be no connection for the pastors between homophobia and sexism. The

38. West, *Disruptive Christian Ethics*, 67.

belief among the pastors is that patriarchy and sexism could be eradicated without consideration of homophobia or heterosexism.

If liberating biblical traditions, regarding the kinship of humankind under God, have comprised a treasury of antislavery apologia in the struggle for Black emancipation in the eighteenth and nineteenth centuries, we have yet to develop a treasury of pro-woman apologia to ensure the full empowerment of Black women in the religious and socio-political spheres of Black culture.[39] It then stands to reason that #BlackLivesMatter presents an opportunity to reshape the narrative and lift the intersectional realities of a large portion of the Black population. Interestingly, as the pastors discussed intersectionality, none of the conversation circled back to equality, justice, or human dignity as it relates to the LGBTQQIA+ community. It is also worth noting, relative to intersectionality, that neither issues of class distinction nor educational opportunity gaps were mentioned during the focus group session.

The pastors saw the movement as an opportunity to unite the Black community, but they really seemed to struggle with how the church would maintain its religious distinction and actively engage the most marginalized of the Black experience. Questions of how transgendered people can be active in the life of the church—without causing upset in the life of traditional families—as it relates to forcing conversations about sex and sexuality that congregants may be unwilling to engage, became the impetus for problematizing the LGBTQQIA+ community in local churches. One pastor lifted the question about the role of the church in society and whether it is an issue of salvation of the soul or salvation of the society. All the pastors agreed that finding common ethical ground is important to the survival of the community and that respect for understood boundaries is essential for the success of any church. As Bishop Yvette Flunder has taught, freedom without responsibility and accountability is as detrimental as slavery.[40] In community, freedom cannot be an end in itself; it must flow from freedom from something to freedom

---

39. Warnock, *Divided Mind of the Black Church*, 141.

40. Flunder, *Where the Edge Gathers*, 12.

for something greater. In the pastor's focus group it seemed that having internalized the standards of the oppressor and adopting the oppressors' guidelines, the pastors themselves were fearful of freedom.[41] The pastors of the focus group showed no capacity to imagine inclusion as a greater way of being. There was no theology of the welcoming table present.

The pastors agreed there is a need to claim explicitly that Black lives are nonthreatening, and recraft the narrative that Black success is a threat to white people. All the pastors reported that their congregations see the current state of police-community relations as a function of white rage in response to the election of President Barack H. Obama and the subsequent appearance of a Black Attorney General. Without exception, the focus group revealed a sense of connectivity to #BlackLivesMatter as resistance to white supremacy and white rage. This is where the pastors had no argument with the #BlackLivesMatter movement. The conversation turned to the historical role of the Black Church as the prophetic voice and moral pulse of America. The Black church was held as the exemplar institution in the Black community to resist the opportunity-hoarding of the dominant culture in ways that further disinherit Black people. Opportunity-hoarding, a practice of the dominant group, keeps good things like education, jobs, and capital within their social network (most often predominantly white). This habitual way of acting reproduces racial disadvantage.[42] The pastors articulated the task of the Black Church as providing Black people with subjectivity and a national identity.

The focus group revealed a renewed passion and admiration for activism. Eighty percent of the pastors felt that #BlackLivesMatter invigorated the millennials in their congregations. The issue that surfaced in response to prophetic praxis was that the same eighty percent of the pastors felt that the church was not welcomed in the #BlackLivesMatter movement—they were not consulted in the planning stages for demonstrations; instead, they were only

41. Freire, *Pedagogy of Freedom*, 47.
42. Glaude, *Democracy in Black*, 60.

approached when the organizers needed a facility. There is an apparent disconnect in the minds of pastors who think in terms of hierarchy and have not fully grasped the organic nature of the leadership model for #BlackLivesMatter. One pastor from St. Louis echoed the general group feeling of alienation from the movement; while this is consistent with other pastors in the group, it is curious in light of other documented research. According to Leah Gunning Francis, clergy people were involved in the Ferguson movement from day one. In her ground-breaking work, Francis interviewed twenty-four local faith leaders who participated in the movement from its inception and who were affiliated with mainline denominations.[43] I cannot fully explain the gap in the historical reality of the movement and the results of the focus group, but a clear divergence exists in the experience of the focus group pastors and, at least, this particular historian's view. Perhaps upon close investigation of the movement I must admit that fewer Black evangelicals were present on the ground floor of the movement and more Black clergy from mainline denominations actively lent their voices. The focus group reveals the ongoing tension between the tradition of the prophetic Black church which focused on issues of marginalization as systemic injustice and evangelical/prosperity gospel churches that see these same issues as primarily behavioral. There is a great conflict regarding the theological, social, and political mission and heart of the church.[44]

The focus group pastors talked at great length about the cost of their involvement with all the tenets of #BlackLivesMatter as well as the cost of dissociating from the movement. For most it came down to a generational divide; aligning with the movement wins the favor of millennials, while disassociating garners favor with the older generation. It becomes even more complex as the discussion moved into church finances—a major area of impact and risk. Since, for all of the pastors present, the millennials in their congregations are not the major financial contributors, the risk of

43. Francis, *Ferguson and Faith*, 4.
44. Fluker, *Ground Has Shifted*, 61–63.

committing to the #BlackLivesMatter movement seemed to far outweigh any benefit of partnering, especially because their own theology and church theology differed from the movement's core tenets in multiple places. The pastors lifted the public castigation of Rev. Jeremiah A. Wright during President Obama's first presidential campaign as a prime example of what speaking truth to power risks. Wright was lambasted in the media for preaching Black Liberation theology; he was accused of hating white people and worse. Rev. Wright was right, however, when he proffered that the vicious caricature and political attack on him was, in a real sense, an attack on the Black Church.[45] Many congregations could not withstand that level of public scrutiny of their pastor for a personal conviction that might not align with the majority of the membership base. The pastors seemed to be wrestling with the question of how to respond in real time both to the church and the marketplace in the arena of realpolitik that is in tension with the theo-logic of their traditions.

SUMMARY

The findings from the survey of theologians point to the liberative lens embedded in the tenets of the #BlackLivesMatter movement. Conducting the focus group with pastors of Black congregations revealed that the puritan heritage of the Black Church, and hence of their congregations, causes them to have friction with the #BlackLivesMatter movement. It seems that in the contemporary Black Church, patriarchal Black leaders, male and female, still see race as the primary oppositional force in Black lives. This thinking of discrimination as a single categorical axis has hindered progress of multiple-burdened people in the Black Church. Many sectors of the Black Church, in comparison to the Black theologians, have let go of the distinct ethical, moral, and spiritual prophetic tradition that for so long had formed the backbone and foundation of Black progress. The gap between the academy and the pulpit

45. Warnock, *Divided Mind of the Black Church*, 147.

seems to threaten the long-term viability of the movement at least as it relates to gaining broad-based support from the Black church establishment. This book lays out where the divergence lies between the theology of the #BlackLivesMatter movement and the clergy responsible for pastoring in the local Black Church context.

CHAPTER 5

CONCLUSIONS

HISTORICALLY, ONE OF THE primary tasks of the Black Church has been to create space where Black people can be passionately human and express their innermost wants and desires.[1] It has been the safe harbor where Black people transcend negative cultural identifications associated with race and/or class while having their own inner desires and spiritual longings affirmed. The Black Church in all of her iterations is a repository of Black cultural identity. As the cultural womb of collective Black communities, the church has traditionally been the source of group identification. The Black Church has provided a constant "clap-back" to the dehumanizing anti-Black images in the dominant society.[2] The lessons from the survey and the focus group reveals that there is a serious divide between the pastors who provide the church with leadership, theologians, and activists with regard to the theology of the #BlackLivesMatter movement. This fact may rupture the safety and tranquility of Black Church space for those who are most marginalized.

While the theologians seem to see the #BlackLivesMatter movement as a cultural response to the gospel, the pastors seem

1. Walton, *Watch This*, 198.

2. Harris, *Ministry for Social Crisis*, 25.

to see it in opposition to the message of the gospel. It is as though there are two separate gospel narratives at work in the life of the Black Church. Theologians appear to cling to the narrative of the nineteenth-century Black Church with its tripartite assignment for the church: (1) *proclaim* the reality of Divine liberation; (2) *participate* actively in the struggle for liberation; and (3) *provide* a visible manifestation that the gospel is a reality.[3] It is as if the theologians are completely unaware that almost all Black Christians are theologically conservative and evangelical *and* are in denial of the effects of Puritanism in the development of the Black Church. There seems to be a failure to move beyond the normative mode of Puritanical discourse and the Calvinist underpinnings so common to the development of the Black Church.[4] Black churches have combined a fervent evangelical theology with a progressive political stance for more than one hundred years. At the same time most theological liberals—who see themselves as politically liberal, including Black and womanist theologians—are scornful and dismissive of evangelical Christianity, preferring to interpret the mission and message of Jesus solely in terms of the language and politics of inclusion.[5]

The pastors seem to have shifted to a late twentieth-century model that sees the role of the church as facilitating economic enterprise. The rise of televangelism, and its effects on the local assembly, suggest the idea that the Black Church should focus on experiential encounters with the divine that suspend the material world and the necessity for justice and equality for all at the welcome table.[6] Results of the focus group indicate that Black theology has become too identified with universities and seminaries, at the expense of identification with the Black Church. As far back as the early 1990s scholars and cultural critics were warning the church that in order for liberative theology as a whole

---

3. Warnock, *Divided Mind of Black Church*, 88.

4. Kornegay, *Queering of Black Theology*, 58–61.

5. See Sanders, "Problem of Irrelevance," 73–82.

6. Walton, *Watch This*, 91.

to have a greater impact on the church, the gap between academe and the pew must be closed.[7]

Many of the focus group pastors seem to have been impacted by white culture's gaze and the historic exploitation of Black sexuality. While the theologians may have decolonized their minds, the pastors' responses to their theological posturing seems to be firmly rooted in the Western Christian tradition's purity notions. The effects of imperialist, white-supremacist, capitalist, heteropatriarchy on Black spirituality can never be understated and appears to have led to a respectability politic in the church that is strangling the church's liberation message. Embracing respectability means engaging a polite pursuit of bourgeois morals embodied in thrift, industry, self-control, piety, and other norms that on the surface seem virtuous, but when contextualized in a raced society, often serve individual betterment at the expense of systemic social change.[8] The manner in which Black women and same-gender loving people are treated in many Black churches reflects a Western Christian traditional notion of women being evil and Black women in particular being Jezebels and seducers of men.[9] There is also the long tradition of seeing LGBTQ persons as sinners, abominations, perverts, and diseased. Black sexuality has been the site of domination and terrorism from the slave era forward and often Black people, particularly in the church, sought to present an image of respectability in order to attain the benefits of full citizenship. From the time of J. Edgar Hoover, antiracist advocates like Bayard Rustin and James Baldwin were targeted for their sexuality. The FBI worked tirelessly to ensure that antiracist activities and gayness were seen as interconnected threats to national security.[10] It would seem that whole segments of the Black Church are still wrestling with oppression sickness; that is, the internalized oppression that causes the oppressed to be infected by the sickness of the oppressor. Any time both the oppressed and

---

7. Douglas, *Black Christ*, 87.

8. Fluker, *Ground Has Shifted*, 37.

9. Douglas, *Sexuality and the Black Church*, 46.

10. Mumford, *Not Straight, Not White*, 25.

the oppressor share the same view of the oppressed, liberation is impossible.

Self-hating behavior is not uncommon in oppressed populations. Oppressed individuals often engage with systems that degrade them. In fact, all oppressed people try hard in some stage of liberation to assimilate and prove to the oppressor that they are okay.[11] The effort to mimic the dominant Christian culture still has witness in the Black Church tradition with classism, sexism, heteroprivilege, patriarchy, and ultimately closed doors.[12] It would appear that local congregations, at least in many facets of the Black Church are extremely resistant to any move against heterosexism. LGBTQQIA+ people constitute a radical and despised "other" for many. It is an attitude modeled by white supremacy to see despised others as so different that they are considered less than human.[13] The focus group revealed that the Black Church suffers from the sin of heterosexism and not only homophobia.

Heterosexual supremacy doesn't necessarily advocate the hatred of gay people, but it always advocates heterosexism. This heterosexism manifests in the church, and by the exclusion of nonheterosexually identified persons from leadership roles within the church, and gives space for leaders to practice hate speech from the pulpit that masquerades as preaching. While it was out of the crucible of racial oppression that the Black Church tradition emerged as a nonracist appropriation of the Christian faith, and as such represented the capacity of the human spirit to transcend racism, no such transcendence seems present in at least these Black Church congregations for same-gender loving or transgendered people.[14] There is a failure on the part of many leaders to understand the ways minoritized sexuality disrupts and transforms LGBTQQIA+ people's relationships with the church. While the hermeneutic of liberative interpretation exists

---

11. Griffin, *Their Own Received Them Not*, 194.

12. Flunder, *Where the Edge Gathers*, 6.

13. Edman, *Queer Virtue*, 22.

14. Paris, *Social Teachings of the Black Churches*, 11.

for exploration and use, there seems to be a failure in many congregations to apply this hermeneutic without discrimination.

The findings of the focus group point to a collective ideological hegemony, which is defined as "those systems of practices, meanings, and values that provide legitimacy to the dominant society's institutional arrangements and interest."[15] It is as though the Black Church has become the instrument of oppression for many of the Black bodies it purports to nurture. This places the Black Church completely at odds with the counter-hegemonic #BlackLivesMatter movement. The *imago Dei* in each of us must not be relegated to something essentially human, nor to a way of relating to other humans that is contingent on our ability to transcend difference. If we are to embrace theologically that we are made in the image of God, we must see all humanity in the wholeness of each person's particularities as equally in the image of God. It must bring us to remembrance of the interconnectedness of life both transcendentally and immanently in relationship with all humanity and the whole of creation.[16]

The Kindom of God is neither the thesis of individual enterprise nor the antithesis of collective enterprise, but a synthesis that reconciles the truth of both.[17] The current state of the Black Church is that the theologians and pastors seem to be entirely bifurcated as it relates to the #BlackLivesMatter movement, and may jeopardize the longevity and sustainability of the movement. If a movement is to have sustainability, it must rally people with shared ideas to cooperate in certain actions, to make sacrifices, and to have, to some extent, common symbols or even those rituals fundamental to the very meaning of church.[18] It is clear to me that the divided mind of the Black Church will cause the full development of the movement to be hindered in the larger Black community. The division—between the organic intellectuals we have allowed to pastor in the Black Church tradition and

15. Giroux, *Ideology, Culture*, 40.

16. Lightsey, *Our Lives Matter*, 81.

17. King, *Radical King*, 44.

18. Fromm, *On Being Human*, 58.

the academicians who are our esteemed theologians—seems to have created for us an impossible divide. Since the Black Church traditionally held a place of institutional primacy in the Black community, Black churches have historically been the custodians of Black community values.[19] While the Black Church is not monolithic, the uniqueness of the institution has been the ability to nurture a collective consciousness and communal values. Since Black pastors of these churches have traditionally been the voice of the Black Church, then the pastors have served as the gatekeepers of the morals and ethics of the Black community. The #BlackLivesMatter movement marks a change in that norm and presents the Black Church, its pastors, theologians, and parishioners alike, the opportunity to form a new paradigm for continued relevance. The great divide between the theologian and the pastor nay be caused by the way we have traditionally trained the Black pastor. Black churches have suffered because many of the pastors are not academically trained theologians. Both the theologian and pastor are necessary for balance and vitality in the local church, and much of working theology of the church would be different if the pastors were also theologians. If theologians and pastors alike wish for congregants, and the community at large, to take seriously the issues of religious and social justice, they will have to consider that justice extends beyond race to all forms of oppression and domination. Together, the theological academy and the Black Church parish must realize their shared responsibility to the Black community. Both have an ontological mandate to be good news, a kerygmatic mandate to preach good news, and, above all, a mandate of *diakonia*—to practice good news.[20]

Looking forward, theologians must realize that without the Black Church, Black theology becomes an intellectual discourse irrelevant to the spiritual, social, and political life of Black people.[21] The Black Church will be at its best when it leaves behind

19. Paris, *Social Teachings of the Black Churches*, xii.

20. Hopkins, *Black Faith and Public Talk*, 93.

21. See Sanders, "Problem of Irrelevance," 73–82.

aspirations for respectability that are subject to white patriarchal norms. Respectability aspirations are at base anti-Black, for it is the anti-Blackness of white theological thought that renders Black bodies lascivious, and Black sexuality and gender expressions *a priori* in need of conversion.[22] Theologians must abandon the tendency to follow Paul Tillich's error. While there is much to be admired in his work, Tillich and his fellow academicians remained encapsulated in theological centers of learning while training a generation of clergy. They were what we have come to say of many academicians: pontificating from ivory towers. They remained in these centers of isolation and towers of self-congratulation, talking only to one another, unconcerned about the impact of their concepts on the ordinary believer, the person in the pew, or even the ordained who interacted daily with the people of the pews.[23] Much of what is pressing against the lives of congregants is lost on those who have little interaction with them. Much of the preaching in the local context seems absent of rigorous theological consideration. Both are necessary for the robust life of the church, and #BlackLivesMatter seems to be merging the two without explicit theological language.

Theology and particularly ecclesiology that does not work within the context of the holistic view of reality cannot address the needs of our time.[24] The church is irrelevant if it is so concretized in the modality of ritual and routine that it cannot adapt to the needs of those who it claims to serve. #BlackLivesMatter invites us to explore the aim, structure, and criteria of a theological conversation that arises from an analysis and experience of the movement toward full humanity in the anthropological interactions in and with the world. #BlackLivesMatter offers a theological conversation conceived in the sobriety of tragedy and born of the struggle for freedom and the spirit of hope.[25] The theo-logic that erupts from the #BlackLivesMatter movement owes its

22. Crawley, *Blackpentecostal Breath*, 13.
23. Spong, *Why Christianity Must Change*, 175.
24. McFague, *Models of God*, 14.
25. Marsh, *Beloved Community*, 180.

intellectual origins to thinkers such as James Baldwin whose work in *The Fire Next Time* wrestles with the Black Church and challenges readers to struggle with race, gender, class, and sexuality. This is a theo-logic that is born of a movement. Movements spring out of a shared feeling that becomes shared action. They inspire people to make sacrifices through common symbols and rituals.[26] This movement is prophetic and its theo-logic challenges the status quo even to the point of questioning what qualifies one to be a theologian. There is no way one can talk of this emerging theology without the acknowledgment that it is prophetic praxis at its best.

Black theology may have to be revisited in conversation with womanist and queer theologies to birth a new theology, one no longer rooted in the Exodus narrative but, building on womanist theology, one rooted in the exile narrative of Hagar, who represents the marginalized body in that she is a nonbourgeios, sensuous, and rejected slave body. Hagar is rejected because of her sensuality, sexuality, and slave status due to her nonnormative body. Her choice to survive and thrive is the first step toward liberation from trauma.[27] Hagar's intersectional realities situate her story and that of her son as foundational for an emerging intersectional theology.

The term intersectional is borrowed from a Black feminist critique of antidiscrimination doctrine, feminist theory, and antiracist politics originally authored by Kimberle Crenshaw.[28] Crenshaw's original work focused on the intersection of race and gender as it pertained legally to the ways in which race and gender separate, and yet compound, issues of marginalization. The work also lifts up the extreme and compounded marginalization of race, sex, class, sexual orientation, age, and physical ability. A Black female law professor, Crenshaw points out how the dominant conceptions of discrimination condition us to think about subordination as disadvantage occurring along a single categorical axis. Identity theologies of liberation have heretofore been guilty of the same construct without taking into consideration the ways

26. Fromm, *On Being Human*, 58.

27. Crawley, *Blackpentecostal Breath*, 32.

28. See Crenshaw, "Demarginalizing the Intersection," 139–68.

in which multiply burdened, intersectional realities might impact our words about God and the church. #BlackLivesMatter points to a renewed understanding of the barriers to progress embedded in institutions and ideologies founded on a single cause and category of identity. Intersectional theology takes this work and, in an interdisciplinary tradition, contextualizes its significance in the life of the church.

The hermeneutical circle begins and ends in human experience. Codified tradition both reaches back to roots in experience and is renewed and/or discarded through the examination of experience. This experience includes relationship to the divine, oneself, the community, and the world.[29] The #BlackLivesMatter movement is the experience that provides the hermeneutical lens for a new stream of theology; it is, in the particularities and tenets, an intersectional theology. It analyzes the presuppositions of our faith by pondering our Black Church dogma and doctrine. This new stream of theology arises from the lived experiences of the Black bodies in and out of the Black Church. It is honed and fleshed out in conversation with Black, queer, other-abled, anticapitalistic, and immigrant theologians. It is a queering of Black and womanist theology. To *queer* Black theology is to force the radical potentiality of Black liberation and womanist theologies in their enactment; a fresh modality and way of living the church.[30] It is a theological modality that is in conversation with all laboratory movements with a radical potential that rests on the ability to advance strategically oriented political identities arising from a nuanced understanding of power. It is exposing false binaries and creating a liminal space that allows human flourishing and disallows radical othering. Intersectional theology is rooted in shared marginal relationship to dominant power that normalizes, legitimizes, and privileges the dominating powers.[31] It is the emerging alternative that exposes the weaknesses of the norms that have become the

---

29. Ruether, *Sexism and God Talk*, 13.

30. Crawley, *Blackpentecostal Breath*, 17.

31. Johnson and Henderson, *Black Queer Studies*, 43.

foundation of theological houses too small to hold all the family of God.

The *destabilization* of the God of Exodus and exposing the God of exile might make liberation and love possible for all Black bodies in the oppressed state of disappointment in a never-coming promised land.[32] From slavery forward Black people have used the exodus account as a hermeneutical lens, particularly as we looked for and to leadership that would help recast the narrative of Black experience in America. The woman called Moses, Nat Turner, Fredrick Douglas, W. E. B. Dubois, Marcus Garvey, Malcolm X, Rev. Dr. Martin Luther King Jr., Rev. Jesse Jackson, President Barak H. Obama; these have all been leaders of the Moses archetype. Each one has been some form of deliverer for oppressed and disinherited Black people living under imperialist, white-supremacist, capitalist, heteropatriarchy; and not one has delivered Black people safely to the promised land. Emerging in the Obama administration, which came into being during a failed market economy and a permanent underclass, the #BlackLivesMatter movement signals the call for a theology that embraces exile.

Exile is never a voluntary experience; it is always forced by circumstances outside of a person's or a people's control. It is a forced dislocation into which one enters without any verifiable hope of either a return to the past or a specific new land.[33] Black bodies know at the cellular level the experience of exile. Force in all its brutal expression has been the companion of Black bodies, dislocation has been the soundtrack of our sojourn, and verifiable hope the elusive ghost of our dreams. White intransigence in the form of privatized and state-sanctioned violence has molested every institution of Black life. Exile then seems the perfect place for a people in need of #BlackLivesMatter as a movement to begin the task of constructing a new theological house. To be sure, theology requires a certain fluidity of thought that is initiated by the willingness to suspend our beliefs so that we may pursue

32. Kornegay, *Queering of Black Theology*, 65.

33. Spong, *New Christianity*.

God's truth for our lives.[34] For the Black Church, which has been rooted in the evangelical tradition, an understanding coming out of from Hagar's exile (Gen 21) may provide an authentic liberative lens to unmoor the church from the narrative of imperialist, heteropatriarchal norms that leave so many people in the pew out of the beloved community. The promised land and exodus is exclusive, but Hagar and exile is inclusive. The intrinsic contradiction of the US exportation of capitalism and democracy makes our nation the perfect place for this new theological lens to develop. The strain of riding two horses in different directions has proven this is not promised land for marginalized people and demands we look to a new narrative for the work of salvation. The dominant culture purports to believe in a democratic republic with liberty and justice for all, while simultaneously clinging to a demonic system of white supremacist capitalistic greed. The two streams of consciousness can never be reconciled and need a theology that would provide a path to salvation and wholeness.

The exodus motif brings with it the idea of a chosen people. This is problematic in that for Black people in America that would mean one group is chosen over another. For white America that means God leaves them for the Black slave community. The chosen people narrative has failed this nation miserably. This chosen people narrative sets a false dichotomy and allows single identity markers to become the totality of the human experience. It is as though Blackness or whiteness was the fullness of one's personhood. The chosen people motif in this way only serves to turn the oppressed into oppressors. Forced to limit the exploration of other parts of one's identity, our current theological constructs respond in limited ways to our personhood because it forces us to enter the conversation in light of one particularity or another. The exile motif, on the other hand, promises a God who is with and gives Black people the freedom to claim and name God differently than the Eurocentric God given during the ravages of slavery. God's response to the Hagar story in the Hebrew scriptures is not

---

34. Lightsey, *Our Lives Matter*, 68.

liberation. God participates in Hagar's and her child's survival.[35] The exile motif demands that both the robes of academe and the pulpit work together to frame a theology that accounts for the identity of all the Kindom of God. The Hagar exile narrative allows people to enter the theological conversation in the same way that the female, slave, African, forced surrogate Hagar presents: a whole and entire person who is able to be seen in their fullness by the divine.

The call is for a progressive Christianity to center intersectionality in its biblical interpretations, theologies, and church practices. When we create a singular identity as normative for any liberating theology, we marginalize the intersections of diverse people within a group, who experience oppression in varying ways because of the intersectional realities lived by those who exist under multiple burdens.[36] While liberationist discourse has lifted the declaration of identity as paramount in the struggle toward wholeness for Black sexually minoritized people, racial subordination often proceeds and informs sexual identification.[37] The #BlackLivesMatter movement is at least in the vanguard toward integrating the experience of liberation theology. The opportunity for the Black Church is to further decolonize the ways in which the Black Church, and society as a whole, talks about God, the individual, and the community. Intersectional theology speaks back to the interlocking systems of our nation's politic by lifting the voices of those most marginalized by the insidious nature of imperialist, white-supremacist, capitalist, and heteropatriarchal norms. This intersectional theology is a heuristic constructive theology that engages a hermeneutic of hunger that reads the Bible as an answer to what all forms of oppression bring to bear on human dignity. It has not been suspicion that turns people away from the church; it is hunger that drives them to seek help wherever their rights to have a life are being respected.[38]

35. Williams, *Sisters in the Wilderness*, 3.
36. Kim and Shaw, "Intersectional Theology," lines 9–11.
37. Mumford, *Not Straight, Not White*, 96.
38. Soelle, *Silent Cry*, 48.

Intersectional theology engages a hermeneutic of hunger that realizes theologies develop in response to questions arising out of various but specific intellectual, political, and religious situations.[39] By building an intersectional theology, the Black Church responds theologically to the call for respect and human dignity. Since the Black Church has been the prophetic moral compass of the nation since its inception, it is the rightful mother of a theo-logic that cares for the complexities of the whole of the Kindom of God.

Intersectional theology is not the work of liberal erasure; it is the intentional honoring of the ways in which social systems collude to marginalize, disenfranchise, and disinherit people considered nonnormative by the oppressive social systems of those in power. Racial erasure is the sentimental idea that racism would cease to exist if everyone would just forget about race and see each other as human beings who are the same.[40] This concept of erasure is not limited to race, it has become a sentimentality that moves to make all "otherness" invisible, without considering the systems that problematize difference. Far from erasure, intersectional theology highlights the uniqueness of each person's God-given particularities and the ways each interlocking set of particularity allows the individual to contribute to the flourishing of the whole.

The heartbeat of intersectional theology offers a clarion call for racialized and oppressed Christian identities to examine themselves and their experiences within systems of power, placing complementary, competing, and conflicting voices in conversation with one another as they move together towards social justice as liberating sacred work.[41] The theo-logic of participation and compassion both reimagine and recast ecclesiology as a salvific work that embraces difference and demands social justice. Intersectional theology then fully embodies the prescription of Rev 11:15 and

---

39. Cone, *Said I Wasn't Gonna*, 32.

40. hooks, *Black Looks*, 12.

41. A conversation with Rev. Dr. Patrick Johnson Oliver, a self-identified evangelical theologian, on March 4, 2020, helped unmask the truth of this claim for me.

sees the task of the church to usher in the day when the kingdoms of this world become the Kindom of our Christ.

Intersectional theology is talk about God that doesn't privilege the authoritative universal voice found in Eurocentric theological musing. This theology does not abide an undifferentiated whole that obliterates individuality. The authoritative universal voice usually indicates white male subjectivity masquerading as nonracial, non-gendered, objectivity.[42] Instead this is a theology that sees race as a linguistic tool we use in myriad ways to ascribe meaning to ourselves and others. As it assigns difference and value to varying configurations of race, class, gender, sexuality, etc., it thereby makes race a serviceable theological device.[43] Intersectional theology is a hermeneutical lens based in Hagar's naming of God (Gen 16:13). Hagar is the only person in the Bible attributed with the power of naming God, who has ministered to her and empowered her in her intersectional realities. Hagar's Deity is no longer associated with the God of her oppressors. In naming God, Hagar releases herself from the oppressive gaze and consequence of hegemony.[44] The name of God in Hagar's narrative is "the God who has seen me"—an especially relevant aspect of the story for the present discussion because intersectional theology is about seeing particulars and not homogenizing them. While intersectional theology shares with womanist theology a centering of Hagar and her story, intersectional theology considers the multiple sites of Hagar's marginalization as central to the working of God with Hagar. It also wrestles with Abraham's patriarchy and the unavoidable brokenness patriarchy causes. It features Sarah's anti-woman behavior rooted in her complicity with patriarchy. It sees exile as a function of broken community, and yet allows the individual to find and name God in the midst of systemic brokenness. As a work of disidentification, intersectional theology talks back to dominate ideology and theo-logic without strictly opposing or assimilating to it. It is a discipline that works on and

42. See Crenshaw, "Demarginalizing the Intersection," 139–68.

43. Fluker, *Ground Has Shifted*, 69.

44. Williams, *Sisters in the Wilderness*, 25–26.

against a dominant theology simultaneously. It is a strategy that works to reform theology from within, without buckling under the weight of dominant gaze. From inside the conversation of theology in partnership with the tradition it seeks to elevate the importance of particular struggles of resistance.[45]

Intersectional theology takes seriously a Pentecostal perspective in that it is rooted in the experience of Acts 2. It invites the church to be the place where all people hear collectively the good news, and hear it in a language they can both understand and receive. Since the areas of sex, race, and class are all factors in Pentecost, the powerful use of language as an instrument of freedom is a revolutionary message of good news. The dominant culture has used language to subordinate the majority, but Pentecost upends the norm making language accessible to all. Pentecost is a strategy of exercising voice and promoting representation in such a way that it foretells movements like Black Power and #BlackLivesMatter. Pentecost grounds intersectional theology in that it provides potential for both personal expressions and rich community life. It considers that all genders are filled with God's spirit and that ageism has no place in the beloved community. This is a theology that relishes difference and sees that difference as foundational to the work of the Spirit in the world. By understanding that the realm of God is present in unity, the underlying theo-logic of intersectional theology implicates exclusion and inequality as contrary to gospel narrative. One cannot claim to be Pentecostal and traffic in division, since the very origins of Pentecostalism are found in the unity of diverse people. Imperialist, white supremacist, capitalist heteropatriarchy sits in total opposition to the liberating message of Pentecost, in that Pentecost is an open invitation of full personhood into total embodied fellowship with the divine.

The pneumatological foundation of intersectional theology is rooted in the relation of the Spirit to embodiment. Pneumatology as a relatively new field of inquiry emerged approximately fifty years after the Azusa Street revival, which began in 1906. As an

45. Muñzo, *Disidentification*, 11–12.

outgrowth of the Black-led Azusa Street revival, pneumatology is really a field of inquiry directly related to Black bodies.[46] The pneumatological roots of intersectional theology spring from a Pentecostal principle grounded in the capacity to begin or to demand a new beginning. According to the narrative of Acts 2, 6, and 15 the principle characteristic of the first followers of "The Way" is a reliance on the Spirit to continue to inspire them with new ways of being community, until the community of Judaism, which had been their incubator, could no longer contain them as a religio-social home.

Intersectional theology takes the creation story seriously both as the *ruach* is present in creation and in God's act of breathing and animating man. This animating makes the creativity of spirit an intricate part of a fully human being. Spirit is origin of everything; it is first cause (Gen 1:2). This universal Life and Energy finds an outlet in and through all that is energized.[47] The Holy Spirit's labor in biblical narratives is connected particularly to the invisible world of intangible, but also material, animation. That God breathed into humanity the breath of life (Gen 2:7) as an animating force is central to offering a critical performative intervention into the Western juridical apparatus of violent control, repression, and premature death.[48] For those on the margins breathing is a performative act of resistance against the dominant culture's desire to own and control the embodiment of the marginalized.

Intersectional theology reads John 11:35 (Jesus wept) as instructional for the ways our theo-logic must be constructed. Jesus crying in public grants us a window into how we are to talk through the body. It is a theology grounded in the corporeal rather than the discursive. Compassion shows as witness not because Jesus spoke about compassion, rather because the embodiment of Jesus became the container of compassionate expression. In this moment the body becomes a site of social effect. Solidarity with grief shows up as a bodily experience with its own intellectual

---

46. Crawley, *Blackpentecostal Breath*, 39.

47. Holmes, *Science of Mind*, 35.

48. Crawley, *Blackpentecostal Breath*, 34.

credibility. Expressions of the body hold potential as transgressive and transformative sites of resistance to hegemonic dominance. This flies in the face of Western culture that sees bodily expressions such as crying as mere emotionality devoid of intellectual substance. Intersectional theology is a theology that makes room for experience to speak. Intersectional theologians pursue an epistemology rooted in the body in full acknowledgment of the teaching of John 1:14, that the Word became *flesh*. Intersectional theology is a mode of engagement that gives voice and credence to the lived reality of embodiment.

Intersectional theology interrogates the biblical account of the Ethiopian eunuch whose body was possibly altered to produce a gender nonconforming way of being in the world. The embodiment of the eunuch may have been transgendered or intersex; how the eunuch was queered doesn't in any way alter or lessen the reality of their nonnormative body. The presumption that birth bodies are "how God made you" has negatively affected the day-to-day living of transpersons.[49] When Philip was led by the Spirit to minister to the Ethiopian eunuch, he was not told to heal the man (Acts 8:26–39). Changing of embodiment was not essential to salvation. Because of the queer embodiment of the Ethiopian eunuch, intersectional theology boldly recognizes that gender expression does not always match genital configuration and that for many people these identities do not reinforce one another as expected but rather, challenge the way they are scripted to be performed.[50] In a society that operates in a raced, gendered, sexed, classed hierarchy, intersectional theo-logic provides the spiritual and moral compass to dismantle the prevailing system, forecast, and implement a preferable future.

Because fetishism (an inanimate object worshiped for its supposed magical powers or because it is considered to be inhabited by a spirit) constitutes precisely the most egregious problems for Black bodies in public life, intersectional theology

49. Lightsey, *Our Lives Matter*, 69–70.
50. Buechel, *That We Might Become God*, 7.

radically embraces the lived reality and embodiment of Jesus.[51] The poor Jewish Jesus with his nonnormative body (particularly if one subscribes to the virgin birth or immaculate conception) shows up with an anti-imperialist message over against the religious tradition of his time. It is Jesus who unhinges the relationship between the underprivileged and the privileged: born in a manger and becoming King of the Jews without amassing either wealth or military might. St. Irenaeus of Lyons lays a foundational building block for us in the second century when he postulates that Jesus Christ did, through His transcendent love, become what we are, that He might bring us to be even what He is Himself.[52] It is then impossible to separate the embodiment of Jesus and one's understanding of one's own embodied self. For those who seek and see justice in the Christian faith, the embodiment of Jesus is an inversion of the profane and a valorization of the stigmatized. Intersectional theology gives full attention to the circumcision of Jesus in Luke 2:21 as placing Jesus both in a completely male body and a completely Jewish body. This combination of gender and ethnicity serve to culturally situate Jesus in the human experience. Jesus is the archetypal human (Heb 4:15), just like us, who showed us what the full human might look like if we fully live into it (Eph 4:12–16). Jesus came to show us how to be human—spiritual humans.[53] The cultural situation of the human condition is a matter not to be dismissed theologically as it is centered in the story of Jesus from the beginning. Identity manifests itself in the flesh; and therefore, it has social and political consequences for those who live in that flesh.[54] That Jesus is circumcised brings to light the penis of Jesus which serves in the text to both gender and sexualize a lived reality. Jesus is gendered by the act of circumcision because it is culturally male, and sexed by his penis. While many today traffic in a false dichotomy of spirit and body, intersectional theology invites a unity and wholeness which does not privilege

51. Wallace, *Constructing the Black Masculine*, 20.

52. Irenaeus of Lyons, *Against Heresies*, 554.

53. Rohr, *Universal Christ*, 23.

54. Johnson and Henderson, *Black Queer Studies*, 141.

one over the other. We are not apart from our bodies, rather we live in and through our own embodiment.

Intersectional theology centers the Jesus who is incarcerated and dies in a government-sanctioned execution. Intersectionality casts Jesus in his lived reality as a practicing Jewish insurgent living in a territory controlled by Roman political, military, and economic forces. Insurgency is necessitated by the marginalization of the embodiment of Jesus. Jesus was and remains marked by sex, gender, and sexuality. Jesus, through preaching and practice, in living and behavior performed masculinity in ways that opposed patriarchal expressions of maleness.[55] Jesus' body at resurrection (Mark 16; Matt 28; Luke 24; John 20–21) is not contained by space and time, and yet does not remove itself from them. The body of Jesus not fully vested in the performance of masculinity bows to wash the feet of disciples it will die for hours later. From the posture as foot washer—culturally assumed by women—Jesus rises to become spiritual midwife in a garden of prayer. Betrayal will lead this body to crucifixion where the plea of theodicy will arise as a cry of lament. There the forsaken body of Jesus experiencing social alienation and estrangement for its resistance to a culture of dominance will die a subjugated objectification of the projected fears of those in power. Jesus' body is mysterious; it is not bound by the usual human limitations, but also does not annul them. The resurrected body of Jesus bears the past, as it proceeds into the future, and its physical qualities unfold and are suspended.[56] Jesus in his queer embodiment often postulated as asexual and potentially bisexual (John 13:23; Luke 7:36–50), here is where the Black Church will find the moral fortitude to embrace and empower the least of these. Here in the body of Jesus is the radical insurgency of #BlackLivesMatter.

Intersectional theology asks the church to interrogate the communion table to discover the blessed, broken body of this Jesus (Luke 22). It does not see communion as a post-Jewish re-enactment of the Seder, this is not commemoration of that type.

55. Copeland, *Enfleshing Freedom*, 63.
56. Buechel, *That We Might Become God*, 33.

Here at the table we ingest the Body of Jesus, it becomes a part of our embodiment. The line between the self and the other is broken and we recognize the unity of all life. The elements of bread and wine are life-giving and nurture and sustain us. At the very same time these elements are dangerous and present the opportunity of gluttony and drunkenness. The table of common union thus demands that we deal with the whole embodiment of Jesus and of one another. The invitation to moderate how we take each other in is also a warning regarding the effects of taking one another in. Through this constructive theology we ask the present liberation theologies to make room for all those bodies among the pews who are broken in many places—where systems of oppression have denied their full humanity. Here at the table of common union the transgendered convicted felon finds an ally in the heterosexual disabled Harvard professor because they have each looked into the face of Jesus and recognized their shared marginalization. There is no more line of "us" vs. "them" when we have come to the table to eat the shared body and drink the shared blood of Jesus. The table of God must be inclusive because our community is not founded on our transient desires or on the exclusion of other, but rather on the divine, who calls us to be and to be present. Inclusion is an attribute of God in whom the fullness of being (*pleroma*) exists— unity within incredible diversity.[57] This is not uncommon to the life and work of Jesus who found kinship with a particular woman named Mary who possessed an alabaster box in Mark 14:1–11. This woman of reputation and Jesus have the most intimate exchange which is always the sign of sacred fellowship and marks a shift in their reputations. Both self-understanding and public reputation are impacted when we come into contact with the other. For Christians, identity becomes something that draws us into relationship with others, across the lines of ethnicity, nations, and social status. This is a subversive and transgressive movement that demands courage and risks.[58] All of the intersectional implications of communion show up at the final public ritual when the table is

57. Buechel, *That We Might Become God*, 71.

58. Edman, *Queer Virtue*, 42.

shared with the very one who will betray, it is the open expression of the danger of common union.

The creation narratives of Genesis are both metaphors the ancient Israelite writers gave us ways to point to truths about God, truths too difficult to comprehend fully.[59] In using these metaphorical stories the writers gift us with the knowledge that God uses what appears as a sign for something larger (Rom 1:20). In this way our embodiment does not limit us to its particular reflection of the divine because it points to mystery within the divine too large for us to comprehend. Those who are in-spirited point to the vastness of the divine, the full experience of all components of one's social locations are indeed the blueprint of the divine and as such should be embraced and explored as a gift to all humankind.

The sin of intersectional theology is anything that comes against human flourishing. Sin is then a state of being and not an act of doing. In Paul Tillich's words, sin is ontological, not moral.[60] The human need for power over or the desire for bringing another into a subservient role is the abomination. People who have fallen victim to ableism, sexism, ageism, genderism, poverty, and all the other atrocities perpetuated by imperialist, white-supremacist, capitalist, heteropatriarchy may well be served by a fresh understanding of sin. This fresh look at sin may serve as an antidote to the purity codes of white, middle-class, family values that lift up the norming of white, heterosexual, male, able bodies. Intersectional theology calls sin any idea that devalues or marginalizes another. All forms of supremacy that suggest that one group is inferior or superior to another in anyway is sinful and a breach of connectivity with the divine. The biblical command to love because the nature and essence of God is Love (1 John 4:6 and 8) is central to an intersectional theo-logic; therefore, any expression or action that is unloving of anyone is the epitome of sin. This understanding of sin serves to defy the validation of consumerism, militarism, the

59. Edman, *Queer Virtue*, 43.
60. Spong, *This Hebrew Lord*, 60.

school-to-prison pipeline, rape culture, and every other social evil that manifest as broken connection with the divine.

Salvation in intersectional theology is both to be saved *from* oppressive systems of domination and to be saved *to* self-love and the ethic of neighbor love. Hagar's exile is the freedom from the tyranny and soul murder of forced surrogacy. Hagar's situation is congruent with the marginalization and disenfranchisement of today's poor, the sexually and economically exploited victims of extreme capitalism, as much as it is congruent with single motherhood and racial disinheriting.[61] To divorce civil rights from the evils of environmental concerns is to live in a deadly dualism in which there would be no air to breathe.[62] God is with Hagar in surviving and developing an appropriate quality of life.

To be saved from oppressive systems does not mean to be saved from oppression. Often disenfranchised and marginalized people still suffer from internalized oppression. It is internalized oppression when any group thinks the same way about themselves as the oppressor. This leads to oppression sickness that causes the oppressed to mimic the oppression of the oppressor. The effort to mimic dominant culture has greatly infected the Black Church tradition with classism, sexism, heteroprivilege and more. Unfortunately, inferior-feeling groups often seek to make someone else more inferior.[63] Intersectional theology asks the Black Church to look toward an eschatological moment where the Kindom of God comes for all the wretched of the earth.

The Black Church should be determinative and not reflective of society, especially as it deals with the human body as a theological problem. Birthed as it was in response to white supremacy and hegemony, the Black Church must continue to be a prophetic critique of all systems of domination that oppress and marginalize any and all people. Our thinking as a Black Church has to change. The #BlackLivesMatter movement is proof that it is changing. The DNA of our thinking—those powerful and

61. Williams, *Sisters in the Wilderness*, 4.

62. Townes, *Blaze of Glory*, 58.

63. Flunder, *Where the Edge Gathers*, 6.

pervasive prejudgments based on race, gender, sexuality, and religious constructs that comprise an active epistemic framework affecting what we see and how we engage the world—are all bending toward new realities.[64] All theological construction comes out of, and is shaped by, particulars. Particulars shaping theology include, but are not limited to social, political, economic, cultural, and historical dynamics.[65]

At the beginning of this project I was serving as Bishop of Operations in one organization, Vice President of the United Ecumenical College of Bishops, and a member of the College of Affirming Bishops for the Fellowship of Affirming Ministries. At the conclusion of my research I still hold all these positions but, have been installed as the President of the United Ecumenical College of Bishops, due to the illness and subsequent demise of our former president. I have also been installed as the Dean of the College of Affirming Bishops. These multiple positions allow me influence within several spheres of the Black Church, broader streams of Pentecostalism, and beyond. I am grateful for the opportunity to serve in these capacities. It was my place as a clergyperson that gave me contact and credibility with the pastors I surveyed. I was uniquely positioned as an insider to query and interrogate the ranks of leadership. It is my deep love for and total commitment to the church in all of her resplendent glory that motivates me to continue the work of reconciling her to her highest expression. It is my love of all of the people of God that situates the call to justice. Those on the underside of power and privilege and those at the center of power and privilege alike are in need of being reconciled to Christ through the person and work of Jesus. Authentic theology seeks to comfort and discomfort simultaneously in response to the vast mystery that is God. Articulating an intersectional theology gives me a rubric from which to do the work of justice-making throughout the Black Church. This lens helps me identify the most vulnerable populations in and out of the church in order to partner with them toward full inclusion in the life of the church.

64. Kornegay, *Queering of Black Theology*, 6.

65. See Armour et al., "God," 19–76.

Intersectional theology like #BlackLivesMatter is a response, not an answer. It is a way of connecting the realities of embodiment to the truth of the Christian tradition. Like every theological lens that comes before it and those that it is built upon it fails miserably to communicate the full mystery of the divine. It fails to speak to the whole of the human condition, and is not large enough to even fully express the depth of my personal convictions. It will not represent a whole people. It is fundamentally queer, a moving target that cannot be fully defined. Once fully articulated and defined it will cease to be intersectional theology. While I may represent an intersectional lens, I can read the text and the culture only from my particularity.

Intersectional theology cannot live in the academy or in intellectual pursuits alone; it must take root and grow out of the trenches. It is interventionist in nature, in that it seeks to interrupt the collusion of oppressing systems that support dehumanization. Enacting the theories of intersectional theology must be the work of activists who take up numerous causes, #BlackLivesMatter being one avenue to speak to the marginalization and disenfranchisement that serve ideologies of supremacy. It is a radical work of resisting the terrors that are attached to the values of dominant society. The embodiment of intersectional theology demands participation in politics, education, corporate and private business, nonprofits, and cultural production of all types. The church, in humble dialogue with activists, must co-create a theo-logic aimed at human flourishing across racial, sexual, and class divides. It is developed from, and develops conversation with, the ancient biblical narrative and the act of freeing both the marginalized and the dominator.

The #BlackLivesMatter movement and its intersectional theology now inform my work with the Fellowship of Affirming Ministries and the College of Affirming Bishops. Understanding the ways in which the #BlackLivesMatter movement seeks to decenter the heteropatriarchal narrative in the Black community and within the Black Church helps reform my preaching—starting with my local congregation and moving outward to my national platform. Intersectional theology asks me, as a bishop in the church, to identify its anthropological subject with greater clarity. The voices of these multiply burdened bodies require attention. They have been left out of the theological conversation due to single-identity theologies that mirror the hegemony of other theological streams. The prioritization of identities is a product of segregationist thinking. Single identity markers stand as placeholders to erase the full humanity of marginalized people. Intersectional theology challenges me to provide soul care for the entirety of people's lived experiences and for all sacred individuals. It turns my attention to the struggle of those who believe themselves to be white as they wrestle with decentering whiteness and the responsibility of privilege. Calling for a radial redistribution of wealth based on a redemptive narrative of equality and equanimity becomes necessary in the discussion of soteriology because I am constrained by the gospel of Jesus. The critics of intersectional theology will be many, and our greatest gifts. They will push us to rethink, revise, restate, and reimagine. Intersectional theology will expand and morph and ultimately become more than we can imagine at this time. This project asks me to find and articulate what it means to be human, and human in relationship with the divine. It asks me to engage each individual as made by God, in community; and to live in flexible, resilient, just relationships with others, while being embodied in race, gender, sex, sexuality, and culture.[66]

In our local congregation we have taken on the model of learning to receive from the people. Our theology and preaching is informed by the lived reality of the people I am fortunate enough to minister with and to. The people are teaching me how to read the text, and by their truth and through their embodiment, I am discovering the teachings of Jesus. Learning how identity is constructed through the exchange and collapse of gender, sexuality, class, race, criminality, and other social identity markers helps me understand how the work of Jesus is effective in the lives of individuals who I am called to minister among. I am endeavoring and asking the other bishops over whom I have charge to receive

66. Copeland, *Enfleshing Freedom*, 92.

from the people, not just guide, counsel, or push the people in a certain direction, but to receive from the people themselves the kinds of insights forged by their own embodied wisdom.[67] I endeavor to engage the local church and those national bodies of which I have charge, in the full meaning of human freedom—religious, existential, social, and eschatological—through the preached word and lived community.

67. Buschendorf and West, *Black Prophetic Fire*, 91.

APPENDIX A

CONSENT TO PARTICIPATE IN RESEARCH

TITLE: Liberation Theologies in Action: A Theological Conversation About the #BlackLivesMatter Movement

INVESTIGATOR: Bishop Edward Donalson, III

908 2nd Ave. N.
Kent, WA. 98032
206.714.4730

ADVISOR: Mark Lloyd Taylor, PhD

901 12th Avenue,
Seattle WA 98122-1090
Direct (206) 296–5633

PURPOSE: You are being asked to participate in a research project that seeks to investigate the intersections of Womanist, black liberation, and queer theologies within the #BlackLivesMatter Movement in the U.S. Also, to determine if the theological tenets are viable for the life of the Black Church. You will be asked to participate in a focus group.

SOURCE OF SUPPORT: This study is being performed as partial fulfillment of the requirements for the doctoral degree in ministry at Seattle University.

RISKS: There are no known risks associated with this study. However,participation in this study may have as a risk the emotional trauma associated with recalling racism and police brutality. African American pastors engage this risk daily, and the opportunity to talk in a confidential setting can lessen the burden. Because this is a conference with an emphasis on Pastoral care and development the participants come prepared to discuss the sensitive issues that are standard issues for their profession. Each participant will have access to pastoral care during and after the conference.

BENEFITS: There is a failure of the church to theologically engage contemporary social movements in the social media age, in ways that foster sustainability for generational understanding. This is particularly true in the case of the #BlackLivesMatter movement. As I consider how the church can give specific theological language to the movement that will be sustainable in perpetuity, I am energized by the opportunity to be a part of shaping the conversation that will offer theological significance toward action. This project will be a vehicle to engage The Academy, The Church, and The Public simultaneously around the issue of human rights in a scholarly way.

INCENTIVES: Participation in the project will require no monetary cost to you.

CONFIDENTIALITY: No direct identifiers will be used in gathering the information. There will be no gathering and maintain names for this session and while participants will be informed the session is being recorded no names will be used in transcription. Your name will never be used in any public dissemination of these data. All research materials and consent forms will be stored. Human subjects research regulations require that data be kept for a minimum of three (3) years. When the research study ends, all identifying information will be removed from the data, or it will be destroyed. All of the information you provide will be confidential. However, if we learn you intend to harm yourself or others, we must notify the authorities.

RIGHT TO WITHDRAW: Your participation in this study is voluntary. You may withdraw your consent to participate at any time without penalty. Your withdrawal will not influence any other services to which you may be otherwise entitled.

SUMMARY OF RESULTS: A summary of the results of this research will be supplied to you, at no cost, upon request. 908 2nd Ave N Kent, WA. 98032

VOLUNTARY CONSENT: I have read the above statements and understand what is being asked of me. I also understand that my participation is voluntary and that I am free to withdraw my consent at any time, for any reason, without penalty. On these terms, I certify that I am willing to participate in this research project. I understand that should I have any concerns about my participation in this study, I may call [name of investigator], who is asking me to participate, at [insert phone number.] If I have any concerns that my rights are being violated, I may contact Dr. Michelle DuBois, Chair of the Seattle University Institutional Review Board at (206) 296–2585.

_____

Participant's Signature   Date

_____

Investigator's Signature   Date

APPENDIX A

[Delete the following section if not applicable to your study.]

CONSENT TO USE IDENTIFYING INFORMATION:

I give my permission for my name [include as applicable: image, institution, affiliation, direct quotes, etc.] to be used in any presentations, publications, or other public dissemination of the research findings of this study.

_____

Participant's Signature   Date

APPENDIX B

SLIDE 1

FOCUS GROUP

Liberation Theologies in Action: A Theological Conversation About the #BlackLivesMatter Movement

SLIDE 2

- As a son of the Black church I am highly motivated to contribute to the sustainability of social movements that have high impact on the life of the church. There is a failure of the church to engage theologically contemporary social movements in the social media age, in ways that foster sustainability for generational understanding. This is particularly true in the case of the #BlackLivesMatter movement. As I consider how the church can give specific theological language to the movement that will be sustainable in perpetuity,

I am energized by the opportunity to be a part of shaping the conversation that will offer theological significance.

SLIDE 3

- The task of theology is to critique and revise the language of the church. This includes not only the language of uttered speech but also the language of radical involvement in the world (Cone 1997). Critique of the church is conducted in light of the gospel narrative of the life of Jesus and the tradition of gospel values as seen in the biblical text. As a Bishop in the Lord's Church, the work of doing public theology is a fundamental part of the job. This project will be a vehicle to engage the Academy, the Church, and the Public simultaneously around the issue of human rights. The opportunity for a Bishop (specifically in the Pentecostal tradition) to speak in a scholarly way to a social movement as it is taking shape is an opportunity seldom maximized.

SLIDE 4

- There are thirteen published tenets of the #BlackLivesMatter movement inclusive of, but not limited to: restorative justice, queer affirming, and unapologetically Black. These tenets are well articulated, but do not read as distinctly theological. This project attempts to tease out the operative theology of #BlackLivesMatter and offer the #BlackLivesMatter movement and pastors of local congregations theological vocabulary and concepts to advance its dialogue. I also understand that while these tenets must be articulated in theological terms, if the theological method of Black and Womanist theologians does not provide a bridge between liberationist God-talk and the practice of ministry, numbers of churches will succumb to white evangelicalism with no prophetic action (Buschendorf

2014, Warnock 2014). The relationship between the theological infrastructure of a faith community and its social manifestations is circular, each influencing the other (Warnock 2014). #BlackLivesMatter provides these theologies with a vehicle of active agency in the world.

SLIDE 5

- The purpose of this basic qualitative research study is to articulate the intersections of Womanist, black liberation, and queer theologies within the #BlackLivesMatter movement in the U.S. The particulars of the founders of the movement lend themselves very easily to these theological lenses and the movement that has grown is intentionally inclusive of those who reflect the realities that bring these theological rivers together. #BlackLivesMatter was created by three Black queer women; Alicia Garza, Opal Tometi, and Patrisse Cullors in the wake of the trial of George Zimmerman for the killing of Trayvon Martin (Lightsey 2015).

- The Following information is the combined findings of my own theological reflections and a survey of four theologians academically trained and active in the #BlackLivesMatter movement

SLIDE 6

Tenets of #BlackLivesMatter

DIVERSITY

We are committed to acknowledging, respecting, and celebrating difference(s) and commonalities.

GLOBALISM

We see ourselves as part of the global Black family and we are aware of the different ways we are impacted or privileged as Black folk who exist in different parts of the world.

BLACK WOMEN

We are committed to building a Black women-affirming space free from sexism, misogyny, and male-centeredness.

BLACK VILLAGES

We are committed to disrupting the Western-prescribed nuclear family structure requirement by supporting each other as extended families and "villages" that collectively care for one another, and especially "our" children to the degree that mothers, parents, and children are comfortable.

LOVING ENGAGEMENT

We are committed to embodying and practicing justice, liberation, and peace in our engagements with one another.

RESTORATIVE JUSTICE

We are committed to collectively, lovingly, and courageously working vigorously for freedom and justice for Black people and, by extension, all people. As we forge our path, we intentionally build and nurture a beloved community that is bonded together through a beautiful struggle that is restorative, not depleting.

COLLECTIVE VALUE

We are guided by the fact that all Black lives, regardless of actual or perceived sexual identity, gender identity, gender expression, economic status, ability, disability, religious beliefs or disbeliefs, immigration status, or location.

EMPATHY

We are committed to practicing empathy; we engage comrades with the intent to learn about and connect with their contexts.

QUEER AFFIRMING

We are committed to fostering a queer-affirming net-work. When we gather, we do so with the intention of freeing ourselves from the tight grip of heteronormative thinking or, rather, the belief that all in the world are heterosexual unless s/he or they disclose otherwise.

UNAPOLOGETICALLY BLACK*

We are unapologetically Black in our positioning. In affirming that Black Lives Matter, we need not qualify our position. To love and desire freedom and justice for ourselves is a necessary prerequisite for wanting the same for others.

TRANSGENDER AFFIRMING

We are committed to embracing and making space for trans brothers and sisters to participate and lead. We are committed to being self-reflexive and doing the work required to dismantle cis-gender privilege and uplift Black trans folk, especially Black trans women who continue to be disproportionately impacted by trans-antagonistic violence.

BLACK FAMILIES

We are committed to making our spaces family-friendly and enable parents to fully participate with their children. We are committed to dismantling the patriarchal practice that requires mothers to work "double shifts" that require them to mother in private even as they participate in justice work.

INTERGENERATIONAL

We are committed to fostering an intergenerational and communal network free from ageism. We believe that all people, regardless of age, show up with capacity to lead and learn.

Coined by BYP100. (BlackLivesMatter 2015)

SLIDE 7

- Christian theology is language about God's liberating activity in the world on behalf of God's freedom of the oppressed. Any talk about God that fails to make God's liberation of the oppressed its starting point is not Christian (Cone, Speaking the Truth: Ecumenism, Liberation, and Black Theology 1999)
- This work is done by looking at the praxis of the person Jesus and the values which can be connected with his life and work.

SLIDE 8

- This theology analyzes the condition of Blackness in light of God's revelation in Jesus Christ with the purpose of creating a new understanding of Black dignity among Black people and providing the necessary soul in that people to destroy racism (Cone, Black Theology and Black Power 1997).
- It is the task of Black theology to analysis the Black condition in light of God's revelation in Jesus Christ with the purpose of creating a new understanding of Black dignity among Black people, and providing the necessary soul in that people, to destroy White racism (Cone, Black Theology and Black Power 1997).

SLIDE 9

BLACK LIB 2

- Because #BlackLivesMatter is unapologetically black in that it affirms the collective value of Black embodiment, it is in and of itself a praxis of Black liberation theology. To love and desire freedom for Black people is the lens Black liberation theology seeks to contribute to the field of theological inquiry.

SLIDE 10

WOMANIST THEOLOGY

- Womanist theology asks where is God in the lives of Black women and how do Black women name God (Mitchem 2002).
- All theologizing that gives attention to Alice Walker's definition of Womanism is considered womanist theology. Walker's definition includes being a black feminist as well as a woman who loves other woman, sexually and/or nonsexually. In addition, a womanist is committed to the survival and wholeness of entire people male and female (Walker 1983).

SLIDE 11

WOMANIST 2

- The tasks of Womanist theology are, to claim history; to declare the authority of Black women, men, and children; to learn from the experience of the forbears, to admit shortcomings and errors, and to improve the quality of women's lives (Lightsey 2015)
- As the #BlackLivesMatter movement has been founded by women and seeks to be an affirming space free from sexism, misogyny, and male-centeredness, a theological conversation must turn itself to the contribution of womanist theologians in these very areas.

SLIDE 12

QUEER THEOLOGY

- Queer theology, based on queer theory, is LBGTQ people talking about God in a self-consciously transgressive manner, especially in terms of challenging societal norms about sexuality and gender. It challenges and deconstructs the natural binary categories of sexual and gender identity (Cheng 2011).
- Queer theology postulates that God gives gays and lesbians the rather startling variation of their sexuality to help their brothers and sisters have greater insights into the reality of their God (Empereur 2002).
- While holding homosexuality as a Divine gift, queer theology is inclusive of this gift while not being limited to this gift. Queering, as a theological methodology, is a deconstruction and re-evaluation of gender perspectives that uses as its framework queer theory and as its resources scripture, reason, tradition, and experiences (Lightsey 2015).

SLIDE 13

QUEER 2

- Two of the main tenets of #BlackLivesMatter address the LGBTQ community specifically; any study of the movement in conversation with theology would be diminished and inadequate without a serious consideration of queer theology.

SLIDE 14

WHAT THE THEOLOGIANS SAY

- Seven core theological pillars essential to the historical life of the church support the #BlackLivesMatter movement:
- Equality and Justice
- Imago Dei
- Intersectionality
- Reconciling the whole Black experience and Inclusion
- Marginalization and Disenfranchisement
- Prophetic Praxis and Activism
- Willingness to Risk as Leaders

APPENDIX C

SEVEN PILLARS OF THE #BLACKLIVESMATTER MOVEMENT

Seven Pillars	Respondent 1	Respondent 2	Respondent 3	Respondent 4
Equality and Justice	The #Black-LivesMatter movement compels the faith community to examine the ways unjust discrimination is experienced in the Black community.	Equality among humanity as it pertains to the law and those empowered to enforce the law.		The ascendency of the #BlackLivesMatter movement is situated in a veritable crying of the blood of the martyred from the earth. The three women founders could not turn a deaf ear to those supremely human and humane cries.

Seven Pillars	Respondent 1	Respondent 2	Respondent 3	Respondent 4
Imago Dei	In my view the primary claim of #BlackLives-Matter is God is the creator of all mankind in the image of the Divine.	All life is sacred.	The centering of Black Lives as sacred...essential...not to be ignored in the context of life itself in our global temporal setting.	The being, doing, living and working of the #BlackLivesMatter movement reveals itself as a clear restatement of the inherent sacred worth of Black people (queer, transgender, women, disabled, men, folks with records, Black undocu-mented folks cis-gender folks and those along the gender spectrum). The social media crown jewel was and is an ideological and political intervention stating in bold-lettered relief that God did not create any throwaway Black bodies.

Seven Pillars	Respondent 1	Respondent 2	Respondent 3	Respondent 4
Intersectionality	We cannot speak of restorative justice or call for changed values unless we seek to address the intersectional injustices that impact marginalization and disenfranchisement in myriad ways.	The #BlackLivesMatter movement has the potential to produce theology that is intentional and holistic. . . Womanist evolved because neither Black liberation nor feminism addressed the depth of the nuances the Black female exper-iences.It can be argued that queer theologies are not accountable.	It reveals in theology in the embodiment of the peoples of the movement. Black queer woman-led leadership. . .	Founded by Black queer women committed to the liberation, freedom, and full thriving of Black people. Centering brilliance experi-ence and leadership of women and the unique burdens of women by the continual onslaught upon Black people. Lifting up a practical theology that syncretizes a range of spiritual practice of action events, planning sessions and protests. Speaking from a lexicon of sacred texts that honors and relies upon Black writers,artists, musicians and creators from the ages.

Seven Pillars	Respondent 1	Respondent 2	Respondent 3	Respondent 4
Reconciling and Inclusion		The theological need in the Christian community communion. . .is a call to re-ignite the inclusive Gospel. #BlackLivesMatter is a call to reconciliation within the African American Community.	. . .it is the task of theology today to protect remembering and retelling from suspicion of reductionism and homogenization and to develop their communicative value, indeed superiority for the intercultural exchange." (Unity and Diversity, Metz, 1989) Three duties: **To** protect the narratives from distortion; **To** decode dogmas/theological ideologies that quickly turn into dangerous/erroneous memories/rituals and practices. **To** use the modes of inquiry that highlight the political/historical appropriately	To a large extent it's a living model of this reconciliation. Founded by Black queer women committed to the liberation, freedom and full thriving of Black people.

Seven Pillars	Respondent 1	Respondent 2	Respondent 3	Respondent 4
Marginalization and Disenfranchisement	We cannot speak of restorative justice or call for changed values unless we seek to address the intersectional injustices that impact marginalization and disenfranchisement in myriad ways.	In the social justice era of intersectionality #BlackLivesMatter is perfectly positioned to produce a theology that reaches to the margin of a marginalized people.	The need for honest and rigorous inquiry into race and how it is a determinate factor in our theo-logical lives. . .today! Within black theological circles or mainstream Black Church who make the claims that BLM is of little consequence by their silence or in largely white evangelical settings where only "the gays," abortion and solidarity with the state of Israel are the issues that warrant. . .	

Seven Pillars	Respondent 1	Respondent 2	Respondent 3	Respondent 4
Prophetic Praxis and Activism	My premise is to understand that Jesus' self-identity was in the prophetic tradition of Isaiah. . ..	The directive to the oppressed to rail against injustice. The prophetic tradition is defined by vision that sees and feels change. The oppressed seek freedom because they have a secure vision of change.	In its organizing tactics and strategies. . ."turnup" =direct action, social media, radical confrontation, i.e., this presidential campaign season	This modern day Black social justice movement has awakened a too long dormant faithful response to public policy agendas. The class dynamics and separation within our community and among our churches left a void. #BlackLivesMatter exposed the chasm in stark contrast and demanded action—while not seeking approval or blessing to do so.

Seven Pillars	Respondent 1	Respondent 2	Respondent 3	Respondent 4
Willingness to Risk as Leaders	As with MLK, an inner search and clear answer is advisable. What we are willing to risk to serve the Lord and what are we willing to die for.	African Americans are not quick to take on patriarchy given matters of mass incarceration and police brutality, which is often experienced by men. The community will benefit as we are able to take on the idea of "bruised patriarchy."	Go on board with "turn up" action/activism that contributes to the growth of the movement, not wasting time on the ordinary, mundane to embrace this moment of the extraordinary!!!!	In essence, doing theology within this movement means risking life, limb, and livelihood for the sake of God's kin-dom come. It is a risky place of ministry—serving without thought of personal reward.

BIBLIOGRAPHY

Anderson, Carol. *White Rage: The Unspoken Truth of Our Racial Divide*. New York: Bloomsbury, 2016.

Anderson, Terence R. *Walking the Way: Christian Ethics as a Guide*. Vancouver, BC: United Church, 1993.

Armour, Ellen, et al. "God." In *Constructive Theology: A Contemporary Approach to Classical Themes*, edited by Laural C. Schneider, 19–76. Minneapolis: Fortress, 2005.

BlackLivesMatter. "About Page." www.blacklivesmatter.com/about.

Blank, Hanne. *Straight: The Surprisingly Short History of Heterosexuality*. Boston: Beacon, 2012.

Buechel, Andy. *That We Might Become God: The Queerness of Creedal Christianity*. Eugene, OR: Cascade, 2015.

Buschendorf, Christa, and Cornel West. *Black Prophetic Fire*. Boston: Beacon, 2014.

Cheng, Patrick S. *Radical Love: An Introduction to Queer Theology*. New York: Seabury, 2011.

Clarke, Cheryl. "The Failure to Transform: Homophobia in the Black Community." In *Home Girls: A Black Feminist Anthology*, edited by Barbara Smith, 190–201. New Brunswick, NJ: Rutgers University Press, 2000.

Cone, James. *Black Theology and Black Power*. Maryknoll, NY: Orbis, 1997.

———. *The Cross and the Lynching Tree*. Maryknoll, NY: Orbis, 2011.

———. *God of the Oppressed*. Maryknoll, NY: Orbis, 1997.

———. *Said I Wasn't Gonna Tell Nobody: The Making of a Black Theologian*. Maryknoll, NY: Orbis, 2018.

———. *Speaking the Truth: Ecumenism, Liberation, and Black Theology*. Maryknoll, NY: Orbis,1999.

Copeland, M. Shawn. *Enfleshing Freedom: Body, Race, and Being*. Minneapolis: Fortress, 2010.

Crawley, Ashton T. *Blackpentecostal Breath: The Aesthetics of Possibility*. New York: Fordham, 2017.

Crenshaw, Keberele. "Demarginalizing the Intersection of Race and Sex: A Black Feminist Critique of Antidiscrimination Doctrine, Feminist Theory and Antiracist Politics." In *University of Chicago Legal Forum 1*, 139–68. Chicago: University of Chicago, 1989.

Delay, Tad. *Against: What Does the White Evangelical Want*. Eugene, OR: Cascade, 2019.

Douglas, Kelly Brown. *The Black Christ*. Maryknoll, NY: Orbis, 1994.

———. *Sexuality and the Black Church: A Womanist Perspective*. Maryknoll, NY: Orbis, 1999.

DuBois, W. E. B. *The Souls of Black Folk*. New York: Barnes and Noble Classics, 2003.

Dyson, Michael Eric. *The Black Presidency: Barack Obama and The Politics of Race In America*. Boston: Houghton Mifflin Harcourt, 2016.

Edman, Elizabeth M. *Queer Virtue: What LGBTQ People Know About Life and Love and How It Can Revitalize Christianity*. Boston: Beacon, 2016.

Empereur, James L. *Spiritual Direction and the Gay Person*. New York: Continuum, 2002.

Farley, Wendy. *Tragic Vision and Divine Compassion: A Contemporary Theodicy*. Louisville: John Knox, 1990.

Fluker, Walter Earl. *The Ground Has Shifted: The Future of the Black Church in Post-racial America*. New York: New York University Press, 2016.

Flunder, Yvette A. *Where the Edge Gathers: Building a Community of Radical Inclusion*. Cleveland: Pilgrim, 2005.

Francis, Leah Gunning. *Ferguson and Faith: Sparking Leadership and Awakening Community*. St. Louis: Chalice, 2015.

Frazier, Edward F. (and C. Eric Lincoln). *The Negro Church in America*. New York: Schocken, 1974.

Freire, Paulo. *Pedagogy of Freedom: Ethics, Democracy, and Civic Courage*. Lanham, MD: Rowman & Littlefield Publishers: 2000.

Fromm, Erich. *On Being Human*. New York: Continuum, 1994.

Garza, Alicia. "A Herstory of the #BlackLivesMatter Movement." https://thefeministwire.com/2014/10/blacklivesmatter-2/.

Giroux, Henry A. *Ideology, Culture, and the Process of Schooling*. Philadelphia: Temple University Press, 1984.

Glaude, Eddie S. *Democracy in Black: How Race Still Enslaves the American Soul*. New York: Crown, 2016.

Griffin, Horace L. *Their Own Received Them Not: African American Lesbians and Gays in Black Churches*. Eugene, OR: Wipf & Stock, 2010.

Gutierrez, Gustavo *A Theology of Liberation*. Maryknoll, NY: Orbis, 1988.

Harris, Forest E., Sr. *Ministry for Social Crisis: Theology and Praxis in the Black Church Tradition*. Macon, GA: Mercer University Press, 1993.

Heagle, John. *Justice Rising: The Emerging Biblical Vision*. Maryknoll, NY: Orbis, 2014.

Heifetz, Ronald A., and Marty Linsky. *Leadership on the Line: Staying Alive Through the Dangers of Leading*. Boston: Harvard Business School, 2002.

Hennelly, Alfred T. *Liberation Theologies: The Global Pursuit of Justice*. Mystic: Twenty Third, 1995.

BIBLIOGRAPHY

Hill Fletcher, Jeannine. *The Sin of White Supremacy: Christianity, Racism, and Religious Diversity in America*. Maryknoll, NY: Orbis, 2017.

Holmes, Ernest. *The Science of Mind*. New York: G.P. Putnam's Sons, 1997.

hooks, bell. *Black Looks: Race and Representation*. Boston: South End, 1992.

———. *Rock My Soul*. New York: Atria, 2003.

———. *Salvation*. New York: William Morrow, 2001.

———. *The Will to Change: Men, Masculinity, and Love*. New York: Washington Square, 2004.

———. *Yearning: Race, Gender and Cultural Politics*. Boston: South End, 1990.

Hopkins, Dwight N. *Black Faith and Public Talk*. Waco, TX: Baylor University Press, 2007.

———. *Introducing Black Theology of Liberation*. Maryknoll, NY: Orbis, 1999.

Irenaeus of Lyons, Saint. *Against Heresies*. South Bend, IN: Ex Fontibus, 2010.

Johnson, E. Patrick, and Henderson, Mae G. *Black Queer Studies: A Critical Anthology*. Durham, NC: Duke University Press, 2005.

Kendi, Ibram X. *How to Be an Antiracist*. NY: One World, 2019.

King, Martin Luther, Jr. *The Radical King*. Edited by Cornel West. Boston: Beacon, 2015.

Kim, Grace Ji-Sun, and Susan M. Shaw. "Intersectional Theology: A Prophetic Call for Change." https://www.huffpost.com/entry/intersectional-theology-a-prophetic-call-forchange_b_58dd823de4bofa4c09598794.

Kornegay, El. *A Queering of Black Theology: James Baldwin's Blues Project and Gospel Prose*. New York: Palgrave Macmillan, 2013.

Lightsey, Pamela R. *Our Lives Matter: A Womanist Queer Theology*. Eugene, OR: Pickwick, 2015.

Lowery, Wesley. *They Can't Kill Us All: Ferguson, Baltimore, and a New Era in Americas Racial Justice Movement*. New York: Little, Brown and Co, 2016.

Manning, Marable. *Living Black History*. New York: Basic Civitas, 2006.

Marsh, Charles. *The Beloved Community: How Faith Shapes Social Justice from the Civil Rights Movement to Today*. New York: Basic, 2005.

McFague, Sallie. *Models of God: Theology for an Ecological, Nuclear Age*. Philadelphia: Fortress, 1987.

McNeal, Reggie. *A Work of Heart: Understanding How God Shapes Spiritual Leaders*. San Francisco: Jossey Bass, 2000.

Migliore, Daniel L. *Faith Seeking Understanding: An Introduction to Christian Theology*. Grand Rapid: Eerdmans, 1991.

Mitchem, Stephanie Y. *Introducing Womanist Theology*. Maryknoll, NY: Orbis, 2002.

Morse, Lyn, and Janice M. Richards. *Qualitative Methods*. Los Angeles: Sage, 2013.

Mumford, Kevin J. *Not Straight, Not White: Black Gay Men from the March on Washington tothe Aids Crisis*. Chapel Hill, NC: University of North Carolina Press, 2016

Muñzo, José E. *Disidentification: Queers of Color and the Performance of Politics*. Minneapolis: University of Minnesota Press, 1999.

Palmer, Parker J. *Healing the Heart of Democracy*. San Francisco: Jossey-Bass, 2011.

Paris, Peter J. *The Social Teachings of the Black Churches*. Philadelphia: Fortress, 1985.

Patton, Michael Q. *Qualitative Research and Evaluation Methods*. Thousand Oaks, CA: Sage, 2002.

Perez, Joe. *Soulfully Gay: How Harvard, Sex, Drugs, and Integral Philosophy Drove Me Crazy and Brought Me Back to God*. Boston; London: Integral, 2007.

Queer Theology. "Home Page." https://www.queertheology.com/.

Rohr, Richard. *The Universal Christ*. New York: Convergence, 2019.

Ruether, Rosemary. *Sexism and God Talk: Toward a Feminist Theology*. Boston: Beacon, 1993.

Sanders, Cheryl J. "The Problem of Irrelevance in Black and Womanist Theologies." In *What Does it Mean to Be Black and Christian: Pulpit, Pew, and Academy in Dialogue*, edited by Forest E. Harris Sr., 2:73–82. Nashville: Townsend, 1998.

Schweiker, William. "Public Theology and the Cosmopolitan Conscience" In *Public Theology for a Global Society: Essays in Honor of Max L. Stackhouse*, edited by Deirdre King Hainsworth, 123–38. Grand Rapids: Eerdmans, 2009.

Sensing, Tim. *Qualitative Research*. Eugene, OR: Wipf & Stock, 2011.

Smith, Mitzi. *Womanist Sass and Talk Back: Social (In)Justice, Intersectionality, and Interpretation*. Eugene, OR: Cascade, 2018.

Soelle, Dorothee. *The Silent Cry: Mysticism and Resistance*. Minneapolis: Fortress, 2001.

Spong, John S. *This Hebrew Lord*. New York: HarperOne, 1993.

———. *A New Christianity For A New World: Why Traditional Faith is Dying and How a New Faith is Being Born*. New York: Harper Collins, 2001.

———. *Why Christianity Must Change or Die*. New York: HarperSanFrancisco, 1998.

Taylor, Keeanga-Yamahtta. *From #BlackLivesMatter to Black Liberation*. Chicago: Haymarket, 2016.

Terrell, JoAnne M. *Power in the Blood? The Cross in the African American Experience*. Eugene, OR: Wipf & Stock, 2005.

Thurman, Howard. *Jesus and the Disinherited*. Boston: Beacon, 1976.

Touré. *Who's Afraid of Post Blackness: What it Means to be Black Now*. New York: Free, 2011.

Townes, Emilie M. *In A Blaze of Glory: Womanist Spirituality as Social Witness*. Nashville: Abingdon, 1995.

Turman, Eboni Marshall. "A Conversation with Dr. Eboni Marshall Turman." New York: Union Theological Seminary, March 5, 2014. https://youtu.be/twqWeJYQTBE.

Vanhoozer, Kevin J., and Owen Strachan. *The Pastor as Public Theologian Reclaiming a Lost Vision*. Grand Rapids: Baker, 2015.

Venable-Ridley, C. Michelle. "Paul and the African American Community." In *Embracing the Spirit: Womanist Perspectives on Hope, Salvation, and Transformation*, edited by Emilie M. Townes, 212–33. Maryknoll, NY: Orbis, 1997.

Volf, Miroslav. *A Public Faith: How Followers of Christ Should Serve the Common Good*. Grand Rapids: Brazos, 2011.

Walker, Alice. *In Search of Our Mothers' Gardens: Womanist Prose*. New York: Harcourt, 1983.

Wallace, Maurice O. *Constructing the Black Masculine: Identity and Ideality in African American Men's Literature and Culture 1175–1995*. Durham; London: Duke University Press, 2002.

Walton, Jonathon L. *Watch This: The Ethics and Aesthetics of Black Televangelism*. New York: New York University Press, 2009.

Warnock, Raphael G. *The Divided Mind of the Black Church: Theology, Piety, and Public Witness*. New York: New York University Press, 2014.

Weekly, R. D. *Homosexianity*. Judah First Ministries, 2009.

West, Traci C. *Disruptive Christian Ethics: When Racism and Woman's Lives Matter*. Louisville: Westminister John Knox, 2006.

Williams, Delores S. *Sisters in the Wilderness: The Challenge of Womanist God-Talk*. Maryknoll, NY: Orbis, 1993.

Wink, Walter. *The Powers That Be: Theology for A New Millennium*. New York: GalileeDoubleday, 1998.

Yarber, Angela, and Cody J. Sanders. *Microaggressions in Ministry: Confronting the Hidden Violence of Everyday Church*. Louisville: Westminster John Knox, 2015.

CPSIA information can be obtained
at www.ICGtesting.com
Printed in the USA
LVHW111655270322
714534LV00002B/360